JN237962

改訂版 ホームステイ英会話
おみやげ本

留学時必携！
英語で伝える
ニッポン

英会話のジオス
GEOS Corporation

はじめに

最近では海外旅行に出かけることは珍しいことではなくなりましたし、何らかの形で海外の学校に通っていたり、また仕事の都合で海外で暮らしている人もたくさんいます。
また日本に居ながらにして外国の方に接する機会も増えています。
このように海外を身近に感じることがよくある昨今、言葉の問題もさることながら日本について質問されて困った、という話を聞くことがあります。
日本の文化はいろいろな形で海外でも紹介されているので、興味を持っている方はたくさんいます。そんな人たちに日本文化を紹介できたらいいと思いませんか？また例え海外に行かなくても日本文化を再発見するために読んでみるのもおもしろいでしょう。
この本では都道府県別の見どころ、日本の伝統文化、食べ物、行事、習慣、文字、おみやげなど事細かにカテゴリーを分けて、きれいな写真やイラストと共にそれぞれを紹介しています。また本文からキーワードを抜き出してあるので自分の言葉で説明したい時に使えます。
海外に「おみやげ」として持って行くのも良し、外国人のお友だちに日本文化を紹介する時にヒントとして使うのも良し、の1冊です。

REGIONS 地域

- CLIMATE 気候 ... 6
- HOKKAIDO 北海道 ... 8
- TOHOKU 東北 ... 8
- KANTO 関東 ... 10
- CHUBU 中部 ... 12
- KANSAI 関西 ... 14
- CHUGOKU/SHIKOKU 中国/四国 ... 16
- KYUSHU 九州 ... 18
- OKINAWA 沖縄 ... 19

TRADITIONS 伝統

- SUMO 相撲 ... 22
- JUDO 柔道 ... 24
- KARATE 空手 ... 24
- KENDO 剣道 ... 25
- UKIYOE 浮世絵 ... 26
- SHODO 書道 ... 28
- KABUKI 歌舞伎 ... 30
- NOH 能 ... 32
- KYOGEN 狂言 ... 34
- NINGYO-JORURI 人形浄瑠璃 ... 36
- KOTO 琴 ... 38
- SHAMISEN 三味線 ... 38
- TSUZUMI/TAIKO 鼓/太鼓 ... 39
- WAKA 和歌 ... 40
- HYAKUNIN ISSHU 百人一首 ... 41
- HAIKU/SENRYU 俳句/川柳 ... 42
- IGO 囲碁 ... 44
- SHOGI 将棋 ... 45
- SHIRO 城 ... 46
- JIIN 寺院 ... 48
- JINJA 神社 ... 50
- JAPANESE GARDENS 日本庭園 ... 52
- TRADITIONAL ARCHITECTURE 伝統建築 ... 56
- KIMONO 着物 ... 60
- CHINA 陶器 ... 64
- LACQUERWARE 漆器 ... 64

3

CHOPSTICKS　箸	65
SADO　茶道	66
IKEBANA　いけ花	68
BONSAI　盆栽	70
SHOGUN　将軍	72
SAMURAI　侍	74
NINJA　忍者	76
GEISHA　芸者	78

MODERN CULTURE　現代文化

HOUSING　住宅	80
INSIDE THE HOUSE　家の中	82
HOT SPRINGS　温泉	84
MANGA　マンガ	86
CHARACTER PRODUCTS　キャラクター商品	87
CELL PHONES　携帯電話	88
PACHINKO　パチンコ	89
KARAOKE　カラオケ	90
SCHOOL LIFE　学校生活	92

FOOD　食べ物

SUSHI　寿司	96
SASHIMI　刺身	98
TEMPURA　天ぷら	100
NABEMONO　鍋物	102
OKONOMIYAKI　お好み焼き	104
YATAI　屋台	106
IZAKAYA　居酒屋	107
SOYBEAN PRODUCTS　大豆製品	108
NOODLES　麺類	110
RICE　米	112
SOUP　汁物	114
PICKLES　漬物	115
BENTO　弁当	116
COMMON INGREDIENTS　一般的な食材	118
SWEETS AND SNACKS　お菓子	120
TEA　お茶	122
ALCOHOL　アルコール	123

YEARLY EVENTS　季節の行事

- SHOGATSU　正月 124
- COMING OF AGE DAY　成人の日 126
- SETSUBUN　節分 127
- VALENTINE'S DAY/WHITE DAY　バレンタインデー/ホワイトデー 128
- HINA MATSURI　ひな祭り 129
- HANAMI　花見 130
- TANGO NO SEKKU　端午の節句 132
- GOLDEN WEEK　ゴールデンウィーク 133
- TANABATA　七夕 134
- OBON　お盆 134
- BON ODORI　盆踊り 135
- HANABI　花火 136
- ENNICHI　縁日 137
- TSUKIMI　月見 138
- SPORTS DAY　体育の日 139
- SHICHI-GO-SAN　七五三 140
- OMISOKA　大晦日 141

LANGUAGE AND CUSTOMS　言葉と習慣

- WEDDINGS　婚礼 142
- PRESENTS　贈り物 144
- JAPANESE WRITING　日本の文字 146
- THE JAPANESE SYLLABARY　五十音表 148
- BASIC JAPANESE PHRASES　簡単な日本語フレーズ 150
- ORIGAMI　折り紙 152

SOUVENIRS　おみやげ

- OMAMORI　お守り 154
- MANEKINEKO　招き猫 154
- DARUMA　だるま 155
- UCHIWA/SENSU　団扇/扇子 156
- WASHI　和紙 158
- NOREN　のれん 158
- TENUGUI　手ぬぐい 159

CLIMATE 気候

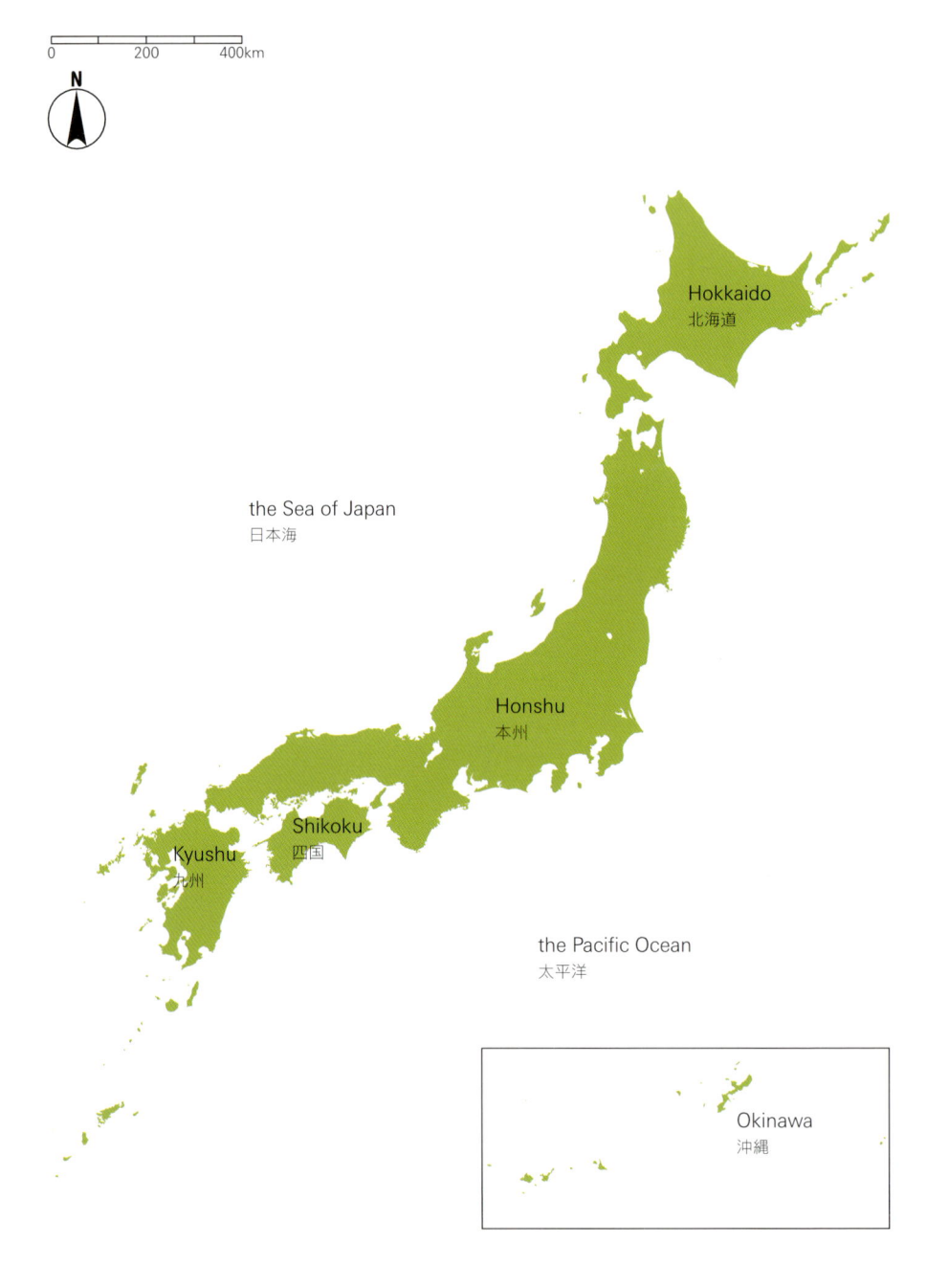

0 200 400km

N

Hokkaido
北海道

the Sea of Japan
日本海

Honshu
本州

Shikoku
四国

Kyushu
九州

the Pacific Ocean
太平洋

Okinawa
沖縄

Japan is a very long country from north to south and has seven main climatic zones: Hokkaido, the northeast, the northwest, the southeast, the southwest and Kyushu. Okinawa, which is several hundred kilometers south of the main islands, also has its own climate.

Hokkaido is dry and cool in summer, and very cold and snowy in winter. The northeast, which faces the Pacific Ocean, is sunny and dry in winter and gets less snow than Hokkaido. The northwest, which faces the Sea of Japan, can get very hot in summer and typically gets lots of snow in winter. The southeast, again facing the Pacific Ocean, is very hot and humid in summer, and dry and sunny in winter. The southwest, again facing the Sea of Japan, has a very mild summer, and gets very cold and snowy in winter. Kyushu the southernmost of the main islands, is hot and wet in summer, and cold in winter. Okinawa is subtropical and warm all year round, but gets a lot of typhoons between July and September.

Between June and July each year, a rainy season blankets all of Japan, except Hokkaido. Typhoons are very common in Japan and several hit or come close to the southern area each year. They are most common in September but can occur at any time. Unlike hurricanes, which are given names, typhoons are numbered. The count starts from one each year.

日本は南北に長くのびた国で、大きく分けて7つの気候帯があります。北海道、北東地域、北西地域、南東地域、南西地域、九州で、沖縄は本土から数百キロ南に位置し、独特の気候です。
北海道は夏は乾燥して涼しく、冬はとても寒く雪がたくさん降ります。北東地域の太平洋側は、冬は晴れて乾燥した日が多く、北海道よりも降雪量が少ないです。北西地域の日本海側は、夏は大変暑くなることもあり冬は豪雪に見まわれます。南東地域の太平洋側は、夏は大変気温が高い上に蒸し暑く、冬は乾燥して晴れた日が多いです。南西地域の日本海側は、夏は穏やかで冬は大変寒さが厳しく雪もよく降ります。日本列島の最南端部を占める九州は、夏は暑くて雨が多く冬は寒いです。沖縄は亜熱帯気候で1年を通して暖かですが、7月から9月にかけてたくさんの台風に見まわれます。
毎年6月から7月には北海道を除く日本列島全体が梅雨に入ります。日本では台風は珍しいことではなく、毎年いくつかが南部に上陸したり接近したりします。台風シーズンは9月ですが年間を通して発生します。ハリケーンには名前がつけられますが、台風には番号がつけられます。毎年1から数えます。

HOKKAIDO/TOHOKU 北海道/東北

HOKKAIDO 北海道

This beautiful island is a popular destination for tourists, who come to see its pristine mountains, forests, meadows, rivers, and lakes. There is a much greater variety of wildlife here than in the rest of Japan, and the seas surrounding the island are clean and beautiful. In addition to tourism, Hokkaido's economy is based on farming, dairy, and various marine industries. Many place-names in Hokkaido are not from Japanese, but from the Ainu language. The Ainu were the original inhabitants of Hokkaido, and are still living there today. They have fought hard to preserve their language and culture, and examples of it can be seen all over Hokkaido.

この美しい島は、手つかずの山々、森、草原、川や湖を見に訪れる観光客に人気のスポットです。日本のどの地域よりもいろいろな野生動物が多く生息し、島を取り囲む海は澄んでいて美しいです。北海道の経済は観光の他に農業、酪農、いろいろな水産業などによって成り立っています。北海道の地名の多くには日本語ではなくアイヌ語に由来するものがあります。アイヌは北海道に元々住んでいた民族で、現在でもこの地に住んでいます。アイヌの人たちは自分たちの言語と文化を守り続け、北海道のあちこちでアイヌ文化を目にすることができます。

TOHOKU 東北

Tohoku is the northernmost region of Honshu. It is not as developed as southern Honshu and its thick forests and tall mountains give it a timeless atmosphere. The rice from this region is of excellent quality and is used to make some of the best sake in Japan.

東北は本州の最北部を占める地域です。本州の南部ほど発展していませんが、深い森と高い山々は時を超えた雰囲気をかもし出しています。この地域の米は品質が高く日本有数の酒の原料にもなっています。

Aomori is famous for its sumo wrestlers, apples and the *Tsugaru jamisen* (see page 38). The highlight of Aomori's Nebuta festival, held at the beginning of August, is the parading of the *nebuta* floats.

1 Hokkaido 北海道
2 Aomori 青森
3 Akita 秋田
4 Iwate 岩手
5 Yamagata 山形
6 Miyagi 宮城
7 Fukushima 福島

1.2. Hokkaido   3. The Nebuta Festival   4. The Kanto Festival   5. The Tanabata Festival

青森県は相撲取り、りんご、津軽三味線が有名です。8月の初めに行われるねぶた祭ではねぶたの引き回しが見物です。

Akita produces some particularly good rice and at the beginning of August the Kanto festival is held to pray for a good rice crop. A *kanto* is a ten-meter pole with 46 paper lanterns hanging from it.

秋田県は特に良質の米の産地として知られ、8月の初めに行われる竿燈まつりは五穀豊穣を祈るためのお祭りです。竿燈は46個の提灯がぶら下がった10メートルほどの竿です。

Iwate is famous for its ironware, called *nanbutetsu*, and for its *wanko soba* restaurants. This is a kind of all-you-can-eat *soba* (see page 110) place where you are served continuous helpings of *soba* in lacquer bowls.

岩手県は南部鉄と呼ばれる鉄器とわんこそば屋が有名です。わんこそば屋は食べ放題のそば屋のようなもので、おかわりのそばがどんどんお椀に入れられます。

Yamagata produces more cherries than any other region of Japan, and is also famous for grapes and pears. Zao, one of the biggest resorts in the Tohoku area, is known for its ski slopes and hot springs.

山形県はさくらんぼの収穫量が日本1で、ぶどうや西洋梨も有名です。東北地方最大級のリゾート地、蔵王はスキー場と温泉で知られています。

Miyagi is just south of Iwate. Prior to the Meiji period (1867-1912), it was one of the richest feudal territories of Japan. In the first week of August, the capital city of Sendai holds the biggest Tanabata festival (see page 134) in all of Japan.

宮城県は岩手県の南にあります。明治時代(1867年〜1912年)以前は日本で最も豊かな藩の1つでした。県庁所在地の仙台では、8月の最初の週に日本で最大規模の七夕祭りが開催されます。

Fukushima is famous for beautiful Lake Inawashiro and Mt. Bandai. It is also known for its Aizu lacquerware.

福島県は美しい猪苗代湖と磐梯山が有名です。会津塗りという漆器も有名です。

写真提供:(社)青森観光コンベンション協会

写真提供:秋田市竿燈まつり実行委員会事務局

写真提供:宮城県観光課

KANTO 関東

KANTO 関東

Kanto is the region around Tokyo. This area of densely populated cities is the political and commercial heart of Japan. However, many of Kanto's historical and cultural features also stand out.

関東は東京周辺の地域です。この人口が密集した地域は日本の政治、商業の中心です。しかし歴史的、文化的な側面も際だっています。

Ibaraki is famous for its research zone, centered on the large collection of labs in the city of Tsukuba. Without a doubt, the best-known food of Ibaragi is *Mito natto* (see page 108), which is popular throughout Japan.

茨城県は研究地域で有名で、中でもつくば市はそういった研究施設の一群の中心になっています。おそらく茨城で1番有名な食べ物は水戸納豆で、これは日本全国で人気があります。

There's a famous shrine called Nikko Toshogu in **Tochigi**. This shrine has a gorgeously carved and painted gate.

栃木県には日光東照宮という有名な神社があります。この神社には非常に豪華な彫刻と彩色が施された門があります。

Gunma is home to one of the great hot springs of Japan. It's called Kusatsu, and it gushes more water than any other hot spring in the country.

群馬県には日本最大の温泉地の1つがあります。そこ、草津温泉は温泉の湧出量が日本1です。

Saitama is filled with cities known as "bed towns" in Japanese. This basically means most of its residents are commuters who spend all day at work (mostly in Tokyo) and come home late at night to sleep.

埼玉県には「ベッドタウン」として知られている町がたくさんあります。「ベッドタウン」とは住民の多くが通勤者で、昼間は大部分が東京で勤め、夜遅くに寝に帰って来る人たちが住む町ということです。

Tokyo, commonly thought of as a city, is actually a prefecture containing several cities. The national government moved to Tokyo in the Edo period (1603-1867), and the Emperor followed in the Meiji period (1867-1912). Tokyo, which used to be called Edo, has been a center of politics, commerce, and culture, for about 400 years. The national government offices and Diet Building (the Japanese parliament) are in Kasumigaseki and Nagatacho respectively. Marunouchi, Otemachi and Shiodome are all centers of business and commerce; and Shinjuku and Shibuya are famous

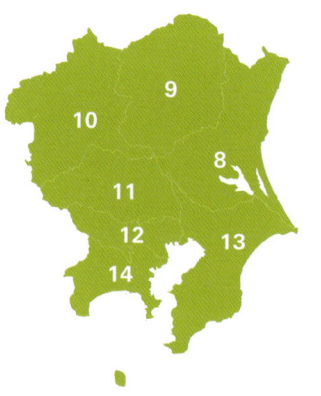

8 Ibaraki
  茨城
9 Tochigi
  栃木
10 Gunma
   群馬
11 Saitama
   埼玉
12 Tokyo
   東京
13 Chiba
   千葉
14 Kanagawa
   神奈川

1. Sensoji temple   2. Tokyo Tower   3. Tokyo Skyline   4. Nikko Toshogu
5. Landmark Tower

shopping districts particularly popular with young people. The atmosphere of the good old days has been somewhat preserved in the area called Shitamachi, where tourists from around the world come to see Sensoji temple in Asakusa and Kokugikan in Ryogoku. Traditional festivals and fairs from the Edo period are still held in this area. Sanno, Sanja, and Kanda, are major festivals in which people parade *mikoshi* (portable shrines) through the streets.

東京都は1つの都市と思われていることが多いですが、いくつかの街によって成り立っています。江戸時代(1603年～1867年)に政府が東京へ移り、明治(1867年～1912年)に入って天皇も移り住みました。東京は昔は江戸と呼ばれ、以来約400年に渡って政治、経済、文化の中心となってきました。日本の省庁や国会議事堂はそれぞれ霞ヶ関と永田町にあります。丸の内、大手町、汐留はビジネスと商業の中心で、新宿、渋谷は特に若者に人気のあるショッピングエリアです。下町には古き良き時代の雰囲気が残っています。世界中からの観光客が浅草の浅草寺や両国の国技館を見に訪れます。この地域では江戸時代からの伝統的な祭りや縁日が今も行われています。山王祭、三社祭、神田祭は御輿を担いで人々が町を練り歩く大きなお祭りです。

Chiba, just east of Tokyo, is home to Narita International Airport, the gateway to Japan. Surprisingly, Tokyo Disneyland is not located in Tokyo at all, but in Chiba.

千葉県は東京のすぐ東に位置し、日本の玄関、成田空港があります。意外にも東京ディズニーランドは東京ではなく千葉にあります。

Kanagawa has two distinct faces, a historical one, and a modern one. The first shogunate (military government) was formed in Kamakura, in southern Kanagawa, about 800 years ago. Many old temples and shrines from that time can still be seen today. The modern face of Kanagawa is represented by Yokohama. It is the second biggest city in Japan and has many great sites, such as China Town, Landmark Tower (the tallest building in Japan), and the Bay Bridge.

神奈川県には歴史的な側面と近代的な側面があります。約800年前に最初の幕府が神奈川県の南部、鎌倉に開かれました。この時代の古い寺院や神社が今日でも多く残っています。神奈川の現代的な側面を代表するのは横浜です。日本第2の大都市で、中華街やランドマークタワー(日本で1番高いビル)、ベイブリッジなどの観光スポットがたくさんあります。

© PART ONE CO.,LTD. 1993

CHUBU 中部

CHUBU 中部

Some of the tallest mountains in Japan are found in Chubu, including glorious Mt. Fuji. This central region of Honshu also contains many hot springs and hot spring resorts.

中部には荘厳な富士山を含む日本で最も高い山々が連なっています。また本州の中心に位置するこの地域には、温泉や温泉リゾートもたくさんあります。

Niigata is famous for its sake, and a brand of rice called *Koshihikari*. Off the coast of Niigata lies Sado island, which was once famous for its gold mines.

新潟県は酒とこしひかりというブランド米が有名です。佐渡島は新潟の沖に位置し、昔は金山で有名でした。

Toyama is well known for its tulips and it exports many bulbs to Europe and North America. Japan's biggest dam is here and attracts many tourists each year.

富山県はチューリップの産地としてよく知られ、ヨーロッパや北アメリカへたくさんの球根を輸出しています。日本最大のダムもあり毎年大勢の観光客を集めています。

Ishikawa was once called Kaga and was one of the richest feudal territories in Japan. Ishikawa is famous for its high quality craftsmanship. For example, *Kaga yuzen* is a dyeing technique often used to create beautiful kimono fabric.

石川県は昔は加賀と呼ばれ、日本で最も豊かな藩の1つでした。石川は品質の高い工芸品が有名です。例えば加賀友禅は美しい着物用の織物を作るのに使われる染めの技法です。

Fukui is famous for marine products like crab and mackerel. Located here is Eiheiji temple, headquarters of the Soto sect of Buddhism. It is a busy monastery with monks and many visitors practicing Zen.

福井県はカニやサバなどの水産物が有名です。この地に建立された永平寺は曹洞宗の大本山です。禅の修行をする僧や訪問者が多数いて、賑わっている僧院です。

Yamanashi is famous for wine and grapes. One of Yamanashi's most beautiful sites is a group of five lakes, called *Fuji goko* (Fuji five lakes). They lie at the foot of Mt. Fuji and are a popular tourist destination.

山梨県はワインとぶどうが有名です。最も美しい観光名所の1つは富士五湖と呼ばれる5つの湖です。富士山の裾野に位置し、人気のある観光地です。

Nagano is probably most famous for its mountains and

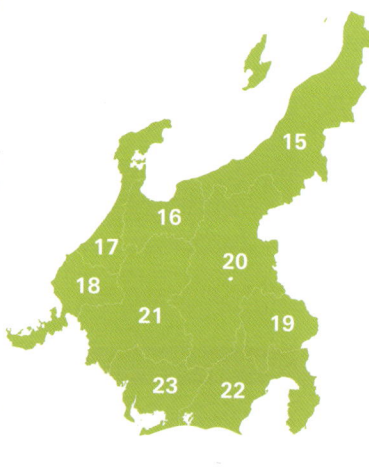

15 Niigata
新潟

16 Toyama
富山

17 Ishikawa
石川

18 Fukui
福井

19 Yamanashi
山梨

20 Nagano
長野

21 Gifu
岐阜

22 Shizuoka
静岡

23 Aichi
愛知

1. Mt. Fuji   2. The Upper Slopes of Mt. Fuji   3. Shirakawago   4. Niigata   5. Nagano

ski slopes. Suwa Shrine is one of the oldest shrines in Japan. The main pillars of each compound are replaced every seven years in a grand festival.

長野県は山とスキー場が大変有名です。諏訪大社は日本最古の神社の1つです。7年毎にそれぞれの建物の支柱が取り替えられる大きなお祭りがあります。

In **Gifu**, there is a famous village called Shirakawago. It consists of about one hundred houses, all of them are more than 100 years old. Amazingly, people still live in these houses. Another town, Takayama also has many houses from the Edo period (1603-1867), and spring and autumn festivals are fantastic.

岐阜県には白川郷という有名な村があります。約100軒の家からなり、そのどれもが築100年以上です。驚くことにまだこれらの家に住んでいる人たちもいます。高山にも江戸時代（1603年〜1867年）からの古い家がたくさん残されていて、春祭りと秋祭りは素晴らしいです。

Izu, in **Shizuoka**, is famous for its hot spring resort areas, such as Ito and Atami. Indeed the regions warm climate has made it a popular choice for health resorts and villas since the old days. Much of Japan's tea comes from Shizuoka as well.

静岡県にある伊豆は伊東や熱海といった温泉地で有名です。温暖な気候なので昔から保養地や別荘地として人気があります。静岡は日本有数のお茶の産地としても有名です。

Nagoya, in **Aichi**, is the fourth biggest city in Japan. It is famous for its castle, which has golden *shachi* (see page 46). Aichi has several specialty foods including *kishimen* (see page 110), *uiro* (steamed jelly made from rice and sugar), *hitsumabushi* (rice with grilled eel), and *tenmusu* (rice balls with tempura).

愛知県にある名古屋市は日本で4番目に大きな都市です。金のしゃちほこがついたお城が有名です。愛知にはきしめん、ういろう、ひつまぶし、天むすなどの名物料理があります。

At 3776 meters, **Mt. Fuji** is the highest mountain in Japan. It stands out clearly because it is much taller than any of the surrounding mountains and is nearly symmetrical. The lower slopes are covered with trees, but the upper slopes are nearly barren.

富士山は3776メートルある日本で1番高い山です。周りの山よりもはるかに高いことと、ほぼ左右対称の形なので際だっています。裾野部分は木々に覆われていますが、上の方の斜面にはほとんど植物が生えていません。

KANSAI 関西

KANSAI 関西

For a long time, Kansai was the political, cultural, and economic center of Japan. Even after the Emperor moved to Tokyo in the Meiji period (1867-1912), many people still felt Kansai was the heart of the nation.

関西は長い間政治、文化、経済の中心でした。明治時代(1867年～1912年)に天皇が東京に移り住んでからも、関西が国の中心であると考えている人はたくさんいました。

Mie is probably most famous for Ise Shrine. This is actually a pair of shrines located several kilometers apart. Both shrines are rebuilt every twenty years. Priests working at these shrines make offerings of vegetables or rice grown on special "sacred" lands nearby.

三重県では伊勢神宮が最も有名です。これは数キロ離れた所に建てられた2つの神社です。どちらの神社も20年毎に建て替えられます。ここで働らく神主は近くの神聖な土地で作られた野菜や米をお供えします。

Shiga holds Japan's biggest lake, Lake Biwa. It's about 672 square kilometers in area. Supposedly, the lake got its name from a musical instrument called a biwa (a stringed instrument) which has a similar shape.

滋賀県には日本最大の湖、琵琶湖があります。面積は約672平方キロです。琵琶という弦楽器に形が似ているのでこの名前がついたと言われています。

Kyoto is famous for many products. *Nishijin-ori* is a type of stiff fabric often used for obi and *Kyo yuzen* is a dyeing technique used for making kimono. Fushimi is known for its sake, and Uji for its tea leaves. The pottery from Kiyomizu is very famous, and the city of Kyoto is renowned for its artistically designed sweets. For more than a thousand years, the Emperor of Japan lived in Kyoto, and many of the temples, shrines, and festivals here are very old. There are three major festivals held in Kyoto each year. They are the Aoi festival on May 15th, the Gion festival from July 17th to 24th, and the Jidai festival on October 22nd.

京都にはいろいろな特産品があります。西陣織は帯によく使われる硬い織物で、京友禅は着物に使われる染めの技法です。伏見は酒、宇治はお茶でそれぞれ有名です。清水焼は大変有名で、芸術的な意匠を凝らした和菓子は名声をはくしています。千年以上の長きに渡って天皇が京都に居を構えていたので、寺院や神社、祭などどれも非常に歴史があります。毎年京都では3つの有名なお祭りが開かれます。5月15日の葵祭、7月17日から24日の祇園祭、10月22日の時代祭です。

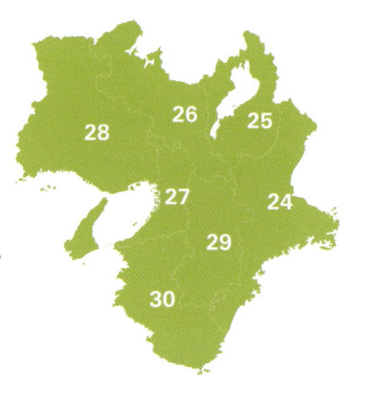

24 Mie
三重
25 Shiga
滋賀
26 Kyoto
京都
27 Osaka
大阪
28 Hyogo
兵庫
29 Nara
奈良
30 Wakayama
和歌山

1. Kyoto 2. Daibutsu 3. Dotonbori 4. Himeji Castle 5. Wakayama

Osaka has been a city of commerce in Japan for a long time, and merchants from Osaka have always been thought to have good business sense. People in Osaka love to eat, and the city's famous Dotonbori district is filled with unique restaurants and delicious food. The most famous festival in Osaka is the Tenjin festival, held on July 24th and 25th.

大阪は長い間日本の商業の中心地で、大阪の商人は商才が非常にあると評価されてきました。大阪の人は食べることが大好きで、有名な道頓堀界隈は独特なレストランやおいしい食べ物であふれています。大阪で1番有名なお祭りは7月24日、25日にある天神祭です。

Hyogo is home to perhaps Japan's most beautiful castle, Himeji Castle. Koshien, the oldest ballpark in Japan, can also be found here. It was built in 1924 and is the site of national high school baseball tournaments every spring and summer. The main city of Hyogo is Kobe. It was a major seaport in the past and has many old Western-style and Chinese buildings.

兵庫県には日本で1番美しいとされる姫路城があります。日本で1番古い野球場、甲子園もあります。1924年に建設され、毎年春と夏には全国高校野球大会の会場になります。兵庫で1番大きな街は神戸です。昔は大きな港町だったので、古い洋風や中国風の建物がたくさん見られます。

Nara was the ancient capital of Japan for most of the eighth century and some of Japan's most impressive temples are here. Todaiji temple is famous for its massive, fifteen-meter tall Buddha (Daibutsu), the largest in Japan. The statue was originally covered in gold, and was consecrated in the year 752 by an Indian monk.

奈良県は8世紀の大半、日本の古い都であったので、大変印象的なお寺のいくつかがあります。東大寺は日本最大15メートルの巨大な大仏で有名です。大仏は元々は金で覆われていて、752年にインドの僧によって開眼供養されました。

Wakayama is home to many important religious places including Mt. Koya and Kumano. These sites are part of a traditional pilgrimage through the Kii Mountains. In the past, many people believed this mountain range to be home to many gods, and it has remained a very spiritual place to this day.

和歌山県には高野山や熊野などの重要な聖地がたくさんあります。これらは紀伊山地の伝統的な巡礼の道の一部です。昔、人々はこの山一帯は神様がたくさん住んでいるところだと考え、今日でも神聖なところとして残されています。

CHUGOKU/SHIKOKU 中国/四国

CHUGOKU/SHIKOKU 中国/四国

This region of Japan includes the southwest tip of Honshu and Shikoku, the smallest of Japan's four main islands. This is also the region in which the Pacific Ocean, Sea of Japan, and Seto Inland Sea meet.

この地域には本州の南西端部と主な4島のうちの1番小さな島、四国が含まれています。ここはまた太平洋、日本海、瀬戸内海が交わる地域でもあります。

Tottori is a small prefecture famous for crabs, shallots, and pears. It also includes the highest mountain in the Chugoku area, Mt. Daisen.

鳥取県はカニ、らっきょう、梨が有名な面積の狭い県です。中国地方最高峰の大山もあります。

Shimane is the setting for one of the great stories from Japanese mythology. It was believed that all the gods of Japan left their homes and moved to Izumo Shrine in Shimane in October of each year. In the rest of Japan, October was known as *Kannazuki*, the month of no gods, but in Shimane it was called *Kamiarizuki*, the month of gods.

島根県は日本の神話でも特に有名な話の1つの舞台となっています。毎年10月には日本中の神様が島根の出雲大社に集まると信じられていました。島根県以外では10月を神無月（神様のいない月）と呼んでいたのですが、島根では神在月（神様のいる月）と呼んでいました。

Okayama is famous for its peaches and muscat, as well as Bizen pottery. This style of pottery is unglazed and has been practiced in the region since the twelfth century.

岡山県は桃とマスカットが有名です。備前焼も有名で、釉薬をかけないこの焼き物は12世紀からここで作られています。

Hiroshima's capital, Hiroshima city, was the site of the world's first nuclear attack. Two sites in the city, The Atomic Bomb Dome and The Peace Memorial Museum, commemorate the victims of the bombing and the desire for everlasting peace. Itsukushima Shrine, on Miyajima island, is considered to be one of the three most beautiful places in Japan.

広島県の県庁所在地、広島市は世界で初めて原爆が投下された町です。原爆ドームと平和記念資料館には原爆によって亡くなった人々を追悼し、恒久平和の祈りが込められています。宮島にある厳島神社は日本三景の1つとされています。

Yamaguchi lies at the western tip of Honshu, many of

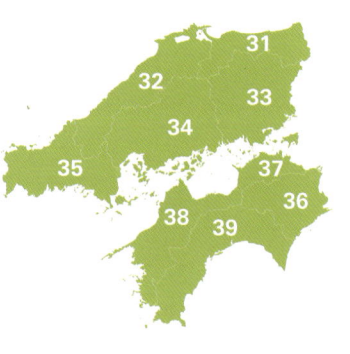

31	Tottori 鳥取
32	Shimane 島根
33	Okayama 岡山
34	Hiroshima 広島
35	Yamaguchi 山口
36	Tokushima 徳島
37	Kagawa 香川
38	Ehime 愛媛
39	Kochi 高知

1. Crabs 2. The Atomic Bomb Dome 3. *Awaodori* 4. Kotohira Shrine
5. The Shimanto River

the talented individuals who established the new government at the end of the Edo period (1603-1867) came from Yamaguchi, including the first Prime Minister, Ito Hirobumi.

山口県は本州の最西端に位置しています。江戸時代(1603年〜1867年)の終わり、新政府の設立に携わった多くの優れた人材を輩出しました。そのうちの1人が初代内閣総理大臣の伊藤博文です。

Tokushima is famous for its traditional dance, *Awaodori*. It can usually be seen during *obon* (see page 134), held between August 12th and 15th. Another major attraction in Tokushima is the Naruto whirlpools. In the channel between Shikoku and Awaji island, rapid tidal currents create these powerful vortices.

徳島県は阿波踊りという伝統的な踊りが有名です。8月12日から15日までのお盆の期間中に開催されます。徳島の他の見どころは鳴門の渦潮です。四国と淡路島の間にある海峡で、潮の流れの速さがこの雄大な渦を作り上げています。

Kagawa's main attraction is Kotohira Shrine, a shrine high up in the mountains. Visitors must climb about eight hundred stone steps to reach it. In the town nearest Kotohira Shrine is the oldest surviving kabuki theater in Japan. It is called *Kanamaru-za* and was built in 1835.

香川県の見どころは山の高いところにある金刀比羅宮です。参詣者は800段ほどの石段を登らなければ神社にたどり着けません。金刀比羅宮の近くには日本最古の歌舞伎専用劇場があります。この金丸座は1835年に造られました。

Ehime is home to one of the oldest hot springs in Japan, Dogo. Its main building was constructed over one hundred years ago, though the spring is said to be three thousand years old.

愛媛県の道後には日本最古の温泉の1つ、道後温泉があります。本館の建物は100年以上前に建てられたものですが、温泉自体は3千年の歴史があると言われています。

Kochi contains the Shimanto River, which is said to be the last clean river in Japan. Surprisingly, many of the bridges crossing the river don't have guardrails or handrails. This allows flood debris to flow over or under the bridges without causing damage.

高知県には日本最後の清流と言われる四万十川があります。驚くことにここにかかる橋の多くには欄干がありません。こうすることで洪水の時に橋を壊すことなく、がれき類を流すことができるのです。

写真提供：金刀比羅宮

写真提供：高知県四万十川流域振興室

KYUSHU/OKINAWA 九州/沖縄

KYUSHU 九州

Kyushu is the farthest south of Japan's four main islands. It has long been a cultural and economic crossroads between Japan and the Asian mainland.

九州は日本列島の主な4島のうち1番南に位置します。長年に渡って日本とアジアの大陸部とを結ぶ文化と経済の中心地でした。

Fukuoka's capital, Fukuoka city, is the largest city of Kyushu. It contains Hakata, which has been an important port for centuries. Every May, people dress up and dance around the city for the Hakata Dontaku festival.

福岡県の県庁所在地、福岡市は九州最大の都市です。ここには何世紀にも渡って重要な港町であった博多があります。毎年5月には博多どんたくが開かれ多くの人々が衣装をまとって町中を踊り歩きます。

Saga is a well-known pottery producing region of Japan and also holds many marine resources. The Ariake Sea is particularly famous for *nori* (see page 118).

佐賀県は陶器の産地として有名で、水産資源も豊かです。有明海は特にのりの産地として有名です。

Nagasaki's capital, Nagasaki city, is another important port. During Japan's prolonged period of isolation Nagasaki was the only port to remain open to the outside world. Every October 7th, a three-day festival called Nagasaki Kunchi is held.

長崎県の県庁所在地、長崎市もまた重要な港町です。日本の長い鎖国の間、長崎港だけが海外に開かれていました。毎年10月7日から長崎くんちと呼ばれる祭りが3日間開かれます。

Kumamoto is called the land of fire. It is home to Mt. Aso, one of the largest active volcanoes in the world. There are many hot springs in the area, and beautiful grassy fields around the mountains.

熊本県は火の国と呼ばれています。熊本には世界有数の活火山、阿蘇山があります。温泉もたくさんあり、山の周辺には美しい草原が広がっています。

Oita is home to many popular hot springs, including Yufuin and Beppu. The water of one of Beppu's hot springs is the color of blood.

大分県には湯布院や別府などよく知られた温泉がいくつもあります。別府温泉には血のように赤いお湯の温泉もあります。

Miyazaki is an important agricultural region of Japan

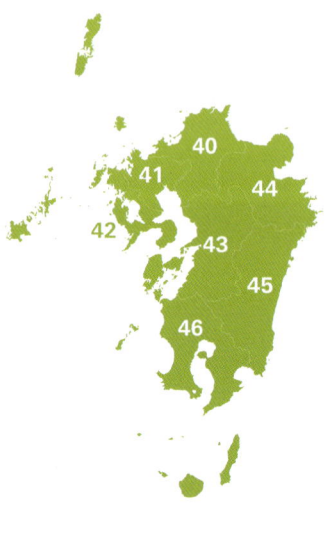

40 Fukuoka
福岡
41 Saga
佐賀
42 Nagasaki
長崎
43 Kumamoto
熊本
44 Oita
大分
45 Miyazaki
宮崎
46 Kagoshima
鹿児島
47 Okinawa
沖縄

18

1. Kumamoto 2. Beppu 3. Takachiho 4. Yakushima 5. Okinawa

and produces most of Japan's winter vegetables. There is a beautiful and mysterious ravine in Takachiho which is very popular with tourists.

宮崎県は重要な農業地域で、日本で冬場に消費される野菜の大半を出荷しています。高千穂には観光客に人気のある、美しくて神秘的な峡谷があります。

Kagoshima was known as Satsuma in the past. Many foods have spread to Japan from Satsuma, including *satsuma imo* (sweet potato), *satsuma jiru* (soup), and *satsuma age* (fried fish paste). Sakurajima, a volcanic island which became joined to the mainland, is famous for its smoking crater. Another island, Yakushima, is covered with ancient cedars, some of which are over two thousand years old.

鹿児島県は昔は薩摩と呼ばれていました。薩摩からさつまいも、薩摩汁、薩摩揚げなどの食べ物が日本全国に広まりました。火山島の桜島は以前は島だったのですが、噴火により本土とつながりました。今も煙を吐く噴火口が有名です。屋久島は古代杉で覆われ、樹齢2千年を超える杉もあります。

OKINAWA 沖縄

The **Okinawa** island chain was an independent kingdom up until the seventeenth century. It was called Ryukyu and had its own king who lived in Shuri Castle in Naha. Ryukyu had its own language and customs. Even today many place-names in Okinawa are not Japanese, but Ryukyu. This island chain was also the only traditional Japanese territory to be invaded during World War II. The battle resulted in many casualties on both sides. After the war, Okinawa was governed by the US until 1972. These days, it is a popular destination for tourists who enjoy the warm climate and beautiful beaches.

沖縄諸島は17世紀までは独立した王国でした。その国は琉球と呼ばれ、王様は那覇にある首里城に住んでいました。琉球文化は独自の言語と習慣がありました。今日でも沖縄の多くの地名は日本語ではなく琉球語で表されています。沖縄は第二次世界大戦中に日本で唯一侵攻された地域でもあります。この戦いでは双方に多数の犠牲者を出しました。戦後1972年まで沖縄は合衆国によって統治されました。現在では温暖な気候と美しいビーチを楽しみに多くの観光客が訪れます。

写真提供：高千穂町役場商工観光課

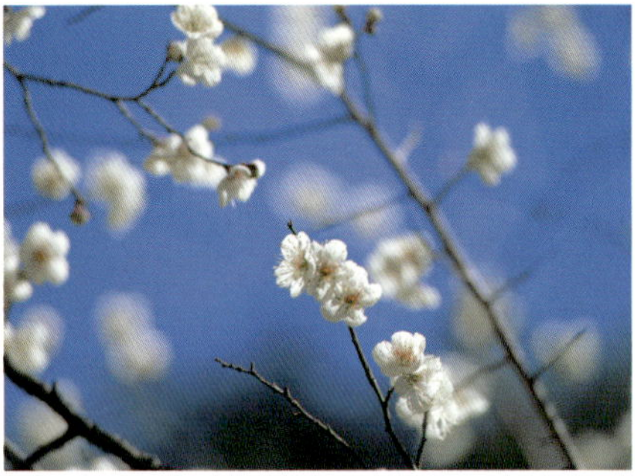
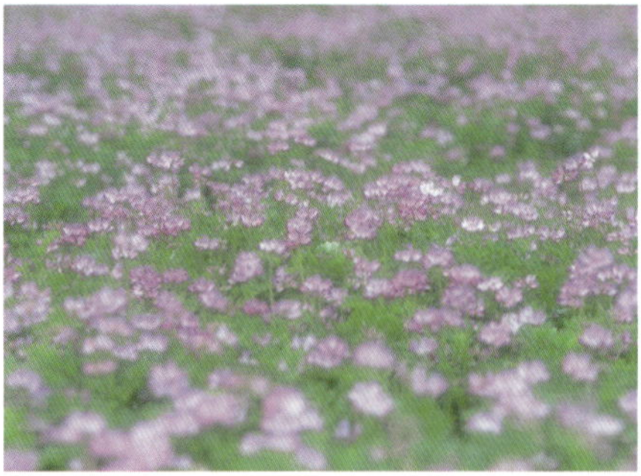
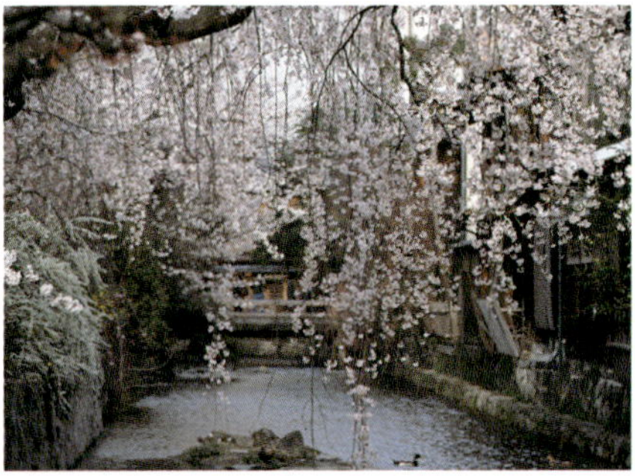
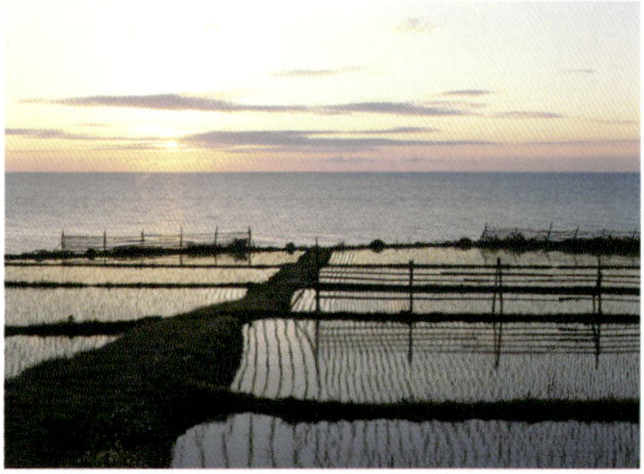
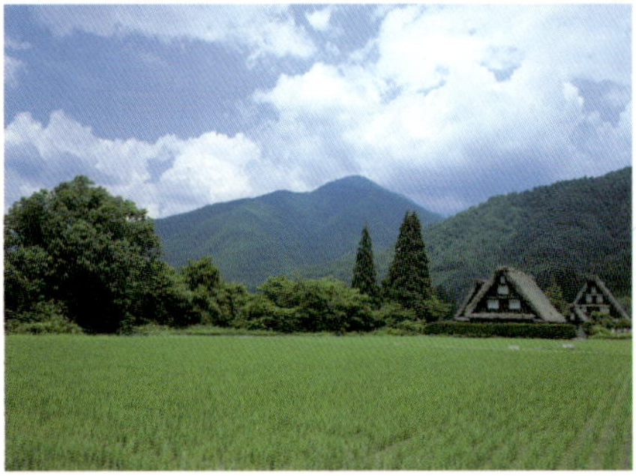
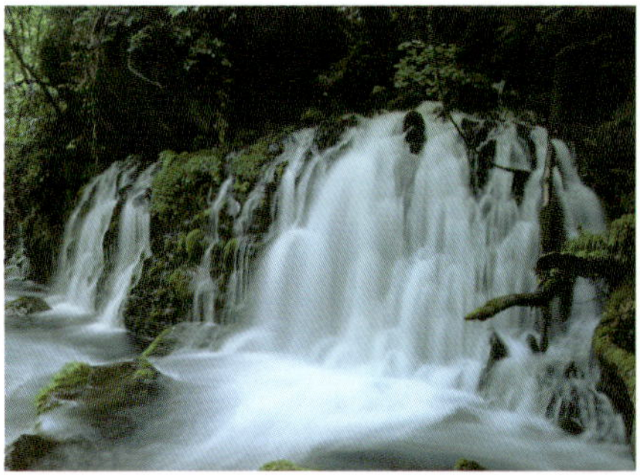
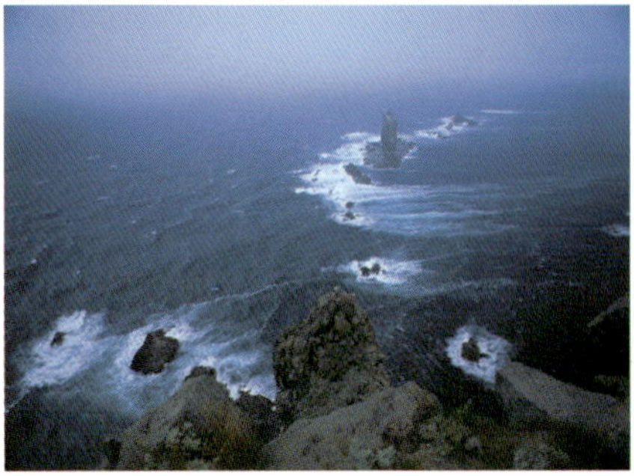
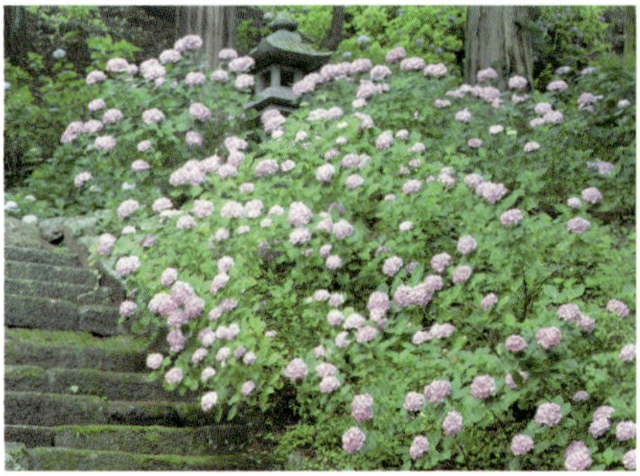

写真提供：四万十市西土佐総合支所

21

SUMO | 相撲

キーワード

national sport	国技
sumo wrestler	相撲取り
have one's hair tied in	髪を〜に結んでいる
topknot	まげ
stand	〜の身長である
opponent	対戦相手
force 〜 to ...	〜に...することを強いる
other than	〜以外の
hold	開催する
last	続く
rank	番付/ランク
determined	決定した
performance	成績
majority	大多数
bout	勝負/試合
demote	降格する
upper division	番付の上位
stable	訓練所/相撲部屋
run	運営する
retired	引退した
rinse	すすぐ
cleanse	清める
throw	まく
ritual	儀式
put up	〜をかける/提供する
prize money	懸賞金
encourage 〜 to ...	〜に...するよう励ます
chant	(大声で)繰り返し言う

Sumo is the national sport in Japan. Sumo wrestlers are called *rikishi*. In the *dohyo* (ring) they wear only a *mawashi* (loin cloth) and have their hair tied in a topknot. The average *rikishi* stands about 1.85 meters tall and weighs around 150 kilos. To win a *rikishi* must push his opponent out of the ring or force a part of his opponent's body (other than his feet) to touch the ground. There are six *hon-basho* (tournaments) each year. Tokyo holds *hon-basho* in January, May, and September, Osaka in March, Nagoya in July and Fukuoka in November. Each *hon-basho* lasts fifteen days. Every *rikishi* has a rank determined by their performance in each *hon-basho*. To move up in the rankings, they must win the majority of their bouts, but if they lose a majority, they are demoted. The highest rank is *yokozuna*, the grand champion, followed by *ozeki*, *sekiwake*, *komusubi* and *maegashira*. These upper division *rikishi* are called *makuuchi-rikishi*, and below them come five more lower division ranks. In recent years, some non-Japanese *rikishi* have reached the highest ranks in sumo, and have brought new excitement and interest to the sport.

相撲は日本の国技です。相撲取りは力士と呼ばれています。土俵の上ではまわしだけを身につけ、髪はまげを結っています。平均的な力士は身長約185センチ、体重は150キロくらいです。対戦相手を土俵の外に押し出すか、相手の体の一部(足以外)を押しやって地面に着かせると勝ちです。毎年6つの本場所が行われます。東京では1月、5月、9月、大阪では3月、名古屋では7月、福岡では11月にそれぞれ行われます。どの場所も15日間続きます。どの力士にもそれぞれの場所の成績によって決められる番付があります。昇進するには勝ち越さなければいけませんし、負け越せば降格します。最高位は横綱で、続いて大関、関脇、小結、前頭の順になります。番付の上位の力士は幕内力士と呼ばれ、下にはさらに5つの番付があります。近年は外国人力士の横綱も誕生し、相撲界に新しい賑わいと関心が寄せられています。

© PART ONE CO.,LTD. 1993

- *Rikishi* belong to stables called *sumobeya* which are run by retired *rikishi*.
  力士は引退した力士が運営する相撲部屋と呼ばれる訓練所に所属しています。
- To enter a *sumobeya*, you must be at least 173 centimeters tall and weigh 75 kilos.
  身長173センチ、体重75キロ以上なければ相撲部屋には入門できません。
- Each *rikishi* has a ring name, called a *shikona*.
  力士には四股名と呼ばれるリングネームがあります。
- *Rikishi* rinse their mouths before each bout to cleanse themselves. Throwing salt on the *dohyo* is another cleansing ritual.
  力士は取り組みの前に水で口をすすいで自分を清めます。塩を土俵にまくのももう1つの清めの儀式です。
- Some companies put up prize money for big sumo bouts.
  大一番には企業からたくさんの懸賞がかけられます。
- The referee, called a *gyoji*, encourages *rikishi* to keep fighting by chanting "*Nokotta, nokotta* (stay in)" throughout each bout.
  行司と呼ばれる審判は取り組みの間中、力士たちに「のこった、のこった」と対戦を続けるように声をかけて励まします。

JUDO 柔道

キーワード
martial art	格闘技/武道
evolve from	～から発展する
originating	起こる
as a form of	～の方法(手段)として
self-defense	護身
value	評価する
moral training	精神的鍛錬
objective	目的
pin	押さえ込む
submit	降参させる
quite	かなり
rough	手荒な
dominate	～で優位を占める
talented	優れた

Judo is both a traditional martial art and a popular sport in Japan. Judo evolved from *jujutsu*, a martial art originating in the eighth century. Judo was developed into a sport by Kano Jigoro in the late nineteenth century. Since then, judo has been used as a form of exercise and self-defense. Many also value it as a form of moral training, especially for children. The objective in judo is to throw your opponent, pin them or force them to submit. During a judo match you may not strike your opponent in any way, so there is no punching, kicking, chopping or hitting of any kind. This is why it is known as "the way of softness," even though it can be quite rough. Judo was introduced to the Olympics at the Tokyo Games in 1964 and has since become a popular event. Although Japan still dominates the sport, several countries are starting to produce very talented *judoka* (judo wrestlers).

柔道は日本では伝統的な武道であり人気のあるスポーツでもあります。柔道は8世紀に始まった柔術から生まれたものです。19世紀の後半に嘉納治五郎がスポーツへと発展させました。それ以来運動や護身術として役立っています。特に子どもにとっては精神的鍛錬になると評価している人もたくさんいます。柔道の目的は対戦者を投げたり、押さえ込んだり、降参するようねじ伏せたりして勝敗を決めます。柔道の試合ではいかなる方法でも相手を打つことは許されないので殴る、蹴る、打つ、叩く、といった攻撃は全くありません。これがかなり手荒なスポーツにも関わらず「柔らの道」として知られているゆえんです。柔道は1964年の東京オリンピックで採用され、それ以来人気のある種目です。まだまだ日本が優位を占めるスポーツではありますが、大変優れた柔道家を輩出する国も出て来ています。

© PART ONE CO.,LTD. 1993

KARATE 空手

キーワード
spread to	～に広まる
be combined with	～と組み合わさる
local	地元の
mainland	本土
style	流派
focus on	～に重点的に取り組む

Thought by many to be a traditional Japanese martial art, karate actually evolved from kung fu (known as *kenpo* in Japan). Kung fu spread to Okinawa, where it was combined with local martial arts to form karate. Karate came to mainland Japan from Okinawa in the early twentieth century and developed into several different styles. Some of these styles are more traditional, focusing on the philosophy of the martial art, while others focus more on the physical side. Karate competitions generally have two events: *kata* (forms) and

philosophy	理念
physical side	身体的な側面
competition	試合
set move	決まった動き
competitor	競技者
specific order	特定の順序
accuracy	正確さ
precision	精度
flow	流れ
intensity	激しさ

kumite (sparring). *Kata* are like martial arts dances. There are set moves that the competitor must complete in a specific order. Accuracy, precision, flow and intensity may all be considered by the judges when scoring *kata*. In sparring matches competitors generally score points by punching or kicking their opponent's body.

伝統的な日本の武道と思っている人が多くいますが、実は空手はクンフー（日本では拳法として知られています）から発展したものです。クンフーは沖縄に広まり、元々沖縄にあった武術と組み合わさって空手が形作られました。20世紀の初めに沖縄から日本本土に伝わり、いくつかの違った流派が生まれました。伝統的で武道の理念に重きを置いている流派もありますが、身体的な側面を重視している流派もあります。空手競技では通常2つの試合があります。型と組手です。型は武道の舞踊のようなものです。決められた動きがあり、選手はそれに応じた順で型を終えなければなりません。型の採点では正確さ、精度、流れ、激しさが評価されます。組手の試合では一般的に対戦者を殴ったり蹴ったりすることで得点が入ります。

KENDO 剣道

キーワード

fencing technique	剣術
warrior	武士
throughout	～の間中
middle ages	中世
middle school	中等学校
refine	磨きをかける
sword	刀
replace	取って代わる
enemy	敵
protective equipment	防具
thigh	腿
quilted panel	キルティングをしたはぎ布

© PART ONE CO.,LTD. 1993

Kendo was the fencing technique used by warriors throughout Japan's middle ages. Today it is a sport practiced by many middle school students (both boys and girls). The basic techniques probably came from China sometime before the tenth century, and were greatly refined by samurai during the Kamakura period (1185-1333). In the early seventeenth century Japan entered a time of peace. Many people still trained in *kendo*, but real swords were replaced by bamboo training swords called *shinai*. These days *kendo* is about exercising the mind and body, not cutting down an enemy, so protective equipment is worn. The face is covered by a mask called a *men*; the body is protected by a chest piece called a *do*; the thighs are protected by quilted panels called *tare*, and the hands are covered by gloves called *kote*.

剣道は中世の時代に武士が行っていた剣術です。今日では男女を問わず多くの学生が稽古しているスポーツです。基本技はおそらく10世紀より以前に中国から伝わったと考えられますが、鎌倉時代（1185年～1333年）に侍によって一段と磨きをかけられました。17世紀の初めに日本は平穏な時代に入りました。依然、剣道で鍛錬をする人も多くいましたが、竹刀と呼ばれる竹でできた練習用の刀が真剣に取って代わりました。今日の剣道は心と体を鍛えるものであって、敵を切るものではありません。ですから防具を身につけます。顔は面と呼ばれるマスクで覆い、体は胴と呼ばれる胸当てで、腿はたれと呼ばれるキルティングをした布で、手は小手と呼ばれるグローブでそれぞれ保護します。

UKIYOE | 浮世絵

キーワード

wood-block prints	木版画
extremely	非常に
art form	芸術スタイル
merchant class	商人階級
prosper	繁栄する
landscape	風景
world-famous	世界的に有名な
subject	題材
remain	今もなお～のままである
favorite	お気に入りの/得意の
theme	テーマ
influence	影響を与える
require	必要とする
carving	彫刻
woodblock	木版

Ukiyoe (wood-block prints) was an extremely popular art form during the Edo period (1603-1867). In this period the merchant class prospered and *ukiyoe* became their favorite art form. *Ukiyoe* often showed images of beautiful women, geisha, kabuki actors and sumo wrestlers, but landscapes and scenes from everyday life were also produced. Several popular images of Japan, such as Mt. Fuji and geisha were first introduced to the world through *ukiyoe*. The *ukiyoe* painter Utamaro is world-famous and he has even been the subject of a movie. *Ukiyoe* pictures remain popular in Japan. They can be seen on postcards, *noren* (see page 158) and other objects.

浮世絵は江戸時代（1603年～1867年）に非常に人気のあった芸術スタイルです。この時代は商人階級が繁栄し、浮世絵は彼ら好みの芸術となりました。浮世絵は美しい女性や芸者、歌舞伎役者、相撲取りだけでなく、風景画や日常生活の様子も描き出しました。富士山や芸者といった日本に対するイメージのいくつかは、浮世絵を通じて初めて世界に紹介されました。浮世絵師の歌麿は世界的に有名で、映画の題材として取り上げられたこともあります。浮世絵は今もなお日本で人気があります。ハガキやのれんや他の商品などで目にすることができます。

Beautiful woman with hand mirror by Utamaro
© PART ONE CO.,LTD. 1993

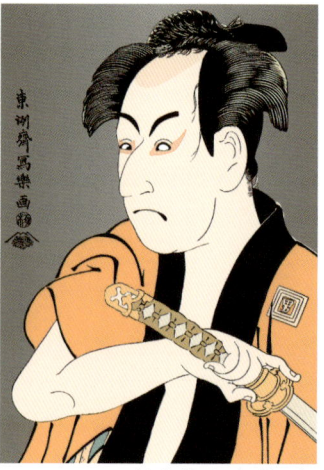

A kabuki actor by Sharaku
© PART ONE CO.,LTD. 1993

The road to Edo by Hokusai
© PART ONE CO.,LTD. 1993

A lake in Hakone by Hiroshige
© PART ONE CO.,LTD. 1993

- Each *ukiyoe* artist had their favorite theme. Utamaro liked painting beautiful women, Sharaku liked actors, and Hokusai and Hiroshige painted scenery.
  浮世絵師にはそれぞれ得意のテーマがありました。歌麿は美人画、写楽は役者、北斎と広重は風景画を好んで描きました。
- *Ukiyoe* art influenced European painters such as Van Gogh.
  浮世絵の画法は、ゴッホなどヨーロッパの画家に影響を与えました。
- Making *ukiyoe* required painting, carving and printing. At least five or six woodblocks were needed for one *ukiyoe*.
  浮世絵は絵描き、彫刻、摺りなどの分業によって作られます。1枚の浮世絵を仕上げるのに木版は最低でも5〜6枚は必要です。

SHODO | 書道

キーワード

calligraphy	書道
spiritual training	精神修行
education	教養
noble	貴族
invent	考案する
simplified	単純化した
running style	くずした字
ornate	凝った
cursive	草書体の
brush	筆
New Year's Card	年賀状
improve	上達させる
handwriting	手書きの文字/筆跡
elementary school	小学校
thin	薄い
rub	する/こする
ink stick	(固形の)墨
ink stone	硯
ready-made	既製の
liquid ink	墨汁

Shodo (calligraphy), which was imported from China, was once one of the arts used in spiritual training and was an important part of the education of Japanese nobles. In the ninth century, *hiragana* (see page 146) was invented. This new writing was much simpler than *kanji* (Chinese characters). As a result, calligraphy became more popular. There are three styles of calligraphy. One is *kaisho*, a square style of writing that anyone can easily read. Another is *gyosho*, a simplified form that is written in a running style. And the final one is *sosho*, a more ornate cursive writing style. It is artistic, but difficult to read. Nowadays Japanese people use pens to write, but many people still enjoy practicing calligraphy and may use a brush and ink to write their New Year's Cards.

書道は中国から伝わり、精神修行の1つとして、また貴族の教養の重要な一部と見なされていました。9世紀にひらがなが考案されました。この書き方は漢字よりもはるかに易しいものでした。このため書道が大変流行しました。書道には3つの書体があります。1つめは楷書で、これは文字の一画一画が明確ですので誰にでも簡単に読むことができます。2つめは行書でくずした文字で書かれる単純化した書体です。3つめは草書で文字をさらにくずした凝った書き方です。これは芸術的ですが読みにくい書体です。現代の日本人は文字を書くのにペンを使いますが、書道の練習を楽しむ人、年賀状を筆と墨で書く人もまだまだたくさんいます。

kaisho   *gyosho*   *sosho*

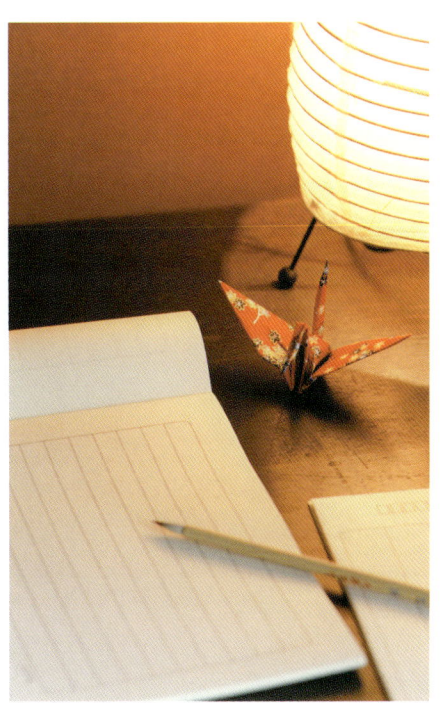

- Many people learn calligraphy, some to improve their handwriting and some just as a hobby.
  多くの人が書道を習っていますが、字がきれいに書けるようになりたい人、単なる趣味としての人など目的はいろいろです。
- Students learn calligraphy at elementary school.
  小学校の授業でも書道を習います。
- There are some calligraphy contests in Japan.
  日本では書道のコンテストがあります。
- Thin Japanese paper called *hanshi* is often used for calligraphy.
  書道には半紙と呼ばれる薄い和紙がよく使われます。
- People used to make ink by rubbing an ink stick against an ink stone, but now, they often use ready-made liquid ink.
  昔は硯で墨をすって墨液を作っていましたが、今は既製の墨汁をよく使います。

KABUKI 歌舞伎

キーワード

originate	始まる
perform	演じる
the very first performance	1番初めの上演
specialize in	～を専門にする
role	役
common people	庶民
be similar to	～に似ている
platform	舞台
extending	のびる
revolving	回転する
lower	降ろす
curtain	幕
eccentric	変わった
original	奇抜な/独創的な
villain	悪人
wig	かつら
stage name	舞台名/芸名
be handed down from generation to generation	受け継がれる 代々
audience	観客
shout out	大声で叫ぶ
applaud	拍手をする

Kabuki is said to have originated in Kyoto with a woman named Okuni at the beginning of the seventeenth century. However, it is now performed only by male actors, so it is amazing that the very first performance was by a woman. Male actors called *onnagata* specialize in playing female roles. Kabuki started out as theater for the common people, so it doesn't have strict rules like noh or traditional Japanese music and dance. The stage was similar to the noh stage at first, but has changed gradually. The *hanamichi* is a platform extending from the main stage. It is used by actors to come and go from the main stage. There's also a revolving stage called a *mawaributai* that can be used to change scenes without lowering the curtains.

歌舞伎は17世紀の初めに阿国という女性が京都で始めたと伝えられています。しかし現在では男優のみが演じているので、1番初めの上演は女性によってされたということには驚かされます。女形と呼ばれる男優が女性の役を専門的に演じます。歌舞伎は庶民向けに始まった演劇ですので、能や他の伝統芸能のように厳しい決まり事はありません。初期の舞台は能舞台と似ていましたが徐々に変化していきました。花道は本舞台からのびている舞台です。役者が本舞台に出入りするのに使います。廻り舞台と呼ばれる回転する舞台装置もあり、幕を引かずに背景を変える時に使います。

© PART ONE CO.,LTD. 1993

- The word kabuki came from *kabuku* which meant eccentric or original.
  歌舞伎は変わっている、奇抜なという意味の言葉、「かぶく」に由来します。
- One make-up style, *kumadori*, uses red make-up for heroes and blue for villains.
  メイク法の一種の隈取は赤系は正義の味方、青系は悪役に使います。
- A kabuki actor's costume and wig can weigh more than sixty kilos.
  役者が身につける衣装やかつらを合わせると60キロを超えることもあります。
- The actor's stage name is handed down from generation to generation.
  役者の舞台名は代々受け継がれていきます。
- The members of the audience shout out their favorite actors' names and applaud when they come on stage.
  ひいきの役者が舞台に出てくると観客が大声で名前を呼んで拍手で迎えます。

NOH 能

キーワード

existing	現存する
nature spirit	自然の精霊
supporting character	サポート役の登場人物(ワキ方)
prop	小道具
abstract	抽象的な
vague	曖昧な
jealousy	嫉妬
portray	表現する
represent	表す
jealous	嫉妬深い
square meters	平方メートル
dressing room	楽屋
pot	かめ
amplify	拡大する
expression	表現
never	決して〜ない
emotion	感情
eye hole	のぞき穴
vision	視界
limited	限られた
mock	見せかけの
hide	隠す
angel's cloak	天女の羽衣
prevent	阻止する
heaven	天

Noh is the oldest existing form of professional theater in the world. It started more than six hundred years ago and is still practiced today. Noh performances use dancing, music, acting and poetry to tell their stories. The main character of each performance is typically a nature spirit or a ghost. Early in the play the spirit meets the supporting character, who is always a man. The supporting character asks about the spirit's story in poetry or song. Few props are used by the actors and the stories are often abstract and vague. The most common story themes are love, jealousy and family. The main actor wears a mask to help portray his character. The most famous of these is the *hannya* mask, which represents a jealous woman. Also on stage, are the musicians and chorus. The stage itself is six square meters and is connected to a dressing room by a bridge. An old pine tree is usually painted on the wall as a background. Pots are placed under the stage to amplify the sound of the actors' footsteps.

能は現存する世界最古の舞台芸術です。600年以上前に始まり現在でも演じられています。能は舞踊、音楽、演技、詩で物語を表現します。どの演目も主人公のほとんどは自然の精霊か幽霊です。芝居の初めで精霊はサポート役の登場人物と出会います。この人物はいつも男性で、精霊の物語を詩や歌で問いかけます。役者はほとんど小道具を使わず、物語はたいてい抽象的で曖昧です。共通する物語のテーマの多くは愛、嫉妬そして家族です。主役は登場人物の役柄を表現するための面をかけます。最も有名な面は嫉妬深い女性を表す般若の面です。また舞台上には楽師と唄い手たちもいます。舞台は6メートル四方ほどの大きさで、楽屋とは橋がかりでつながっています。壁には普通は背景として1本の老松が描かれています。舞台の下には役者の足音を拡大するためにかめがいくつか置かれています。

A *koomote* mask

A *hannya* mask

写真提供 左右とも：http://www.nohmask21.com

- The expression "like a noh mask," means a person who never shows their emotion.

  「能面のような」という表現は感情を表に出さない人のことを指します。

- A noh mask has two eye holes, but they are very small so the actor's vision is limited.

  面にはのぞき穴がありますが、非常に小さいので役者の視界は狭いです。

- There are no curtains on noh and *kyogen* stages.

  能狂言の舞台には幕がありません。

- The stage is inside but it has a mock roof.

  屋内に建てられていますが舞台には見せかけの屋根がついています。

- One of the most popular noh plays is *Hagoromo*. It is the story of a fisherman who finds and hides an angel's cloak, preventing her return to heaven.

  能の有名な演目は「羽衣」です。天女の羽衣を見つけた漁師が、彼女を天に帰さないためにそれを隠した物語です。

KYOGEN 狂言

キーワード

source	もと
comic relief	ちょっとした息抜き
servant	従者
accessible	とっつきやすい
energetic	エネルギッシュな
occasionally	時々
tend to	～の傾向がある
expressive	表情の豊かな
style one's hair	髪を整える
protect	守る
trick	だます/たくらむ
pot	つぼ
be full of	～でいっぱいだ
powerful poison	猛毒
in fact	実際は

Kyogen developed at the same time as noh and the two were often performed together. Traditionally, *kyogen* plays are performed between noh plays. They are generally funny and easy to understand, and so provide a good source of comic relief between the more serious noh plays. These days *kyogen* is much more popular than noh and is often performed separately. The characters are usually a master and his servants, and the story is typically about the characters' daily lives. *Kyogen* is much more accessible for the audience than noh as the players are more energetic and use easily understood language. Masks are only occasionally worn, but when they are, they tend to be more expressive than noh masks.

狂言は能と同時期に作り出されたもので、またこの2つはよく一緒に上演されました。伝統的には狂言は能の合間に演じられます。狂言は一般的に滑稽で理解しやすいので、厳粛な能の演目の合間のちょっとした息抜きを生みだします。現代では狂言は能よりもはるかに人気があり、能とは別に独立して演じられるようになりました。たいていの場合、登場人物は主人とその従者たちで、典型的な物語は登場人物の日常生活を描いたものです。狂言は役者の動きがエネルギッシュで、わかりやすい言葉を使うので、観客にとっては能よりもずっととっつきやすいです。面はあまりかけませんが、狂言の面は能面よりも表情が豊かです。

- *Kyogen* actors always carry a fan on stage. The fan is used as a prop.
  狂言師は舞台に出る時には必ず扇子を持ちます。扇子は小道具として使われます。
- *Kyogen* actors don't wear make-up or style their hair.
  狂言師は素顔で舞台に立ち、髪もそのままです
- One of the most famous *kyogen* plays is *Busu*. It is a comedy about a master who tries to protect his food by tricking his servants. He tells them that a pot in his house is full of powerful poison called *busu*, but in fact it's full of sugar.
  狂言の最も有名な演目の1つは「附子」です。主人が従者をだまして自分の食べ物を守ろうとする喜劇です。主人は家にあるつぼに入っている食べ物は猛毒の附子だと偽りますが、実際は砂糖でいっぱいです。

A noh and *kyogen* stage

NINGYO-JORURI｜人形浄瑠璃

キーワード

puppet	操り人形
meant for	〜のために作られた
at one's peak	絶頂期で
approximately	おおよそ
puppeteer	操り人形師
be visible to	〜に見える
hooded	頭巾をかぶった
mixture of ~ and ...	〜と...を混ぜ合わせたもの
finely	細かく
crushed	砕いた
shell	貝殻
glue	にかわ/のり
surface	表面
porcelain	陶磁器
depending on	〜に合わせて/〜によって
be adopted	取り入れられる
likewise	同様に
love suicide	心中
tragic	悲劇的な
prostitute	遊女
commit suicide	自殺する

A *ningyo-joruri* performance is a puppet show. *Ningyo* means puppet, and *joruri* is a kind of musical story. *Joruri* music is played with the *shamisen* (see page 38). The story, usually meant for adults, is told through *joruri* and the actions of the puppets. This art form was at its peak during the Edo period (1603-1867). All the characters in the story are usually voiced by a single narrator, known as the *tayu*. Each of the approximately one-meter tall puppets is controlled by three puppeteers. The master puppeteer controls the head and right arm of the puppet, and is sometimes visible to the audience. The other two puppeteers control the left arm and legs of the puppet. They are usually dressed in black and hooded, essentially invisible to the audience. The three puppeteers work so smoothly together that it seems like the puppet is moving by itself.

人形浄瑠璃は人形劇です。人形は操り人形のことで、浄瑠璃は音楽を伴う物語です。浄瑠璃音楽は三味線で演奏されます。ストーリーはたいてい大人向けに作られていて、浄瑠璃と人形の動きによって語られます。この芸術は江戸時代（1603年〜1867年）に絶頂期を迎えました。物語の登場人物はほとんど1人の太夫と呼ばれる語り手が演じます。約1メートルの人形はそれぞれ3人の人形遣いが操ります。主遣いは頭と右手を操り、観客から姿が見えることもあります。他の2人の人形遣いは人形の左手と両脚を操ります。この人たちは黒衣を着て頭巾をかぶり、観客からは姿が見えないようにしています。3人の息がぴったり合っているので、まるで人形が1人で動いているかのようです。

写真提供：淡路人形座　萩野忠司氏撮影

写真提供：淡路人形座　萩野忠司氏撮影

- The puppets' faces are finished with a mixture of finely crushed shells and glue, creating a smooth surface almost like porcelain.
  人形の顔は貝を砕いて作った粉とにかわで仕上げられてあり、陶磁器のようになめらかです。
- Each puppet's hairstyle and costume are changed depending on its role.
  人形は役に合わせて髪型や衣装を変えます。
- Many *ningyo-joruri* stories have been adopted by kabuki troupes, and likewise many kabuki stories are performed in *ningyo-joruri*.
  人形浄瑠璃のストーリーは歌舞伎に取り入れられ、また逆に歌舞伎のストーリーを人形浄瑠璃に取り入れることもあります。
- One of the most famous stories is *Sonezaki Shinju* (the love suicide in Sonezaki). First performed on May 7th in 1703, it is a tragic love story about a prostitute and a shop worker who commit suicide together in a forest in Sonezaki.
  有名なストーリーの1つは「曾根崎心中」です。1703年5月7日に初演されました。これは曾根崎の森で心中した、遊女と手代との悲恋の物語です。

KOTO 琴

キーワード

stringed instrument	弦楽器
movable	動かせる
bridge	（弦楽器の弦を支える）駒
pick	（弦を弾くためにつける）爪
attach	はめる
thumb	親指
index finger	人差し指
middle finger	中指
pluck	かき鳴らす/弾く
alter	変える
pitch	音の高さ
tone	音質
written score	楽譜

The *koto* is a stringed instrument sometimes called the Japanese harp. These days it typically has thirteen strings. Each string has its own movable bridge. The body of the *koto* is made from wood and is about two meters in length. Playing the instrument requires both hands. Picks are attached to the thumb, index finger, and middle finger of the right hand, and these are used to pluck the strings. The left hand is used to press the strings in order to alter pitch and tone. Originally, there were no written scores for the *koto* but these days *koto* music is written using both Chinese numbers and Western music.

琴は日本のハープと呼ばれることもある弦楽器です。現在の琴は一般的に13弦です。どの弦にもそれぞれに動かせる駒がついています。胴は木製で2メートルほどの長さがあります。琴は両手を使って演奏します。右手の親指、人差し指、中指に爪をはめて弦を弾きます。左手は弦を押さえて音の高さや音質を変えるのに使います。琴には元々は楽譜がなかったのですが、今日では漢数字や西洋音楽の音符を使って書き表しています。

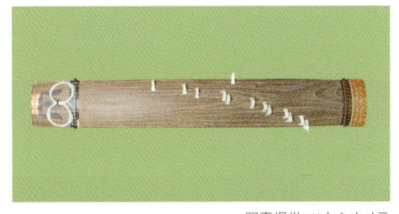

写真提供：ハヤシカメラ

SHAMISEN 三味線

キーワード

variant	変形
vary in	～の点で異なる
thickness	太さ
removable	取り外しのきく
spatula-like	へらのような
plectrum	ばち

The *shamisen* looks a bit like a banjo. It has a square body covered with catskin, with a long neck and three strings. It's usually about one meter in length, but there are some longer variants as well. There are also three different types of neck, which vary in thickness and are sometimes removable. The *shamisen* evolved from an Okinawan instrument called a *sanshin*. It can be played either with a spatula-like plectrum or with the fingers.

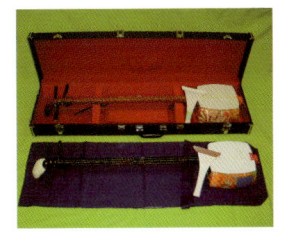

三味線はバンジョーに少し似ています。猫の皮を張りつけた四角い胴と3本の弦を張った長い棹でできています。1メートルほどの長さのものが多いのですが、長い種類のものもあります。棹には3つの種類があり、それぞれ太さが違い、取り外せるものもあります。三味線は沖縄の三線という楽器から発展しました。へらのような形のばちや指を使って演奏します。

写真提供:(株)岡忠

TSUZUMI/TAIKO 鼓/太鼓

キーワード

hourglass-shaped 砂時計の形をした
lacquered 漆塗りを施した
horsehide 馬の皮
lace ひもで締める
tighten しっかり締める
loosen 緩める
cowhide 牛の皮
high-pitched かん高い
barrel 樽

写真提供:(株)岡忠

写真提供:http://www.nohmask21.com

写真提供:http://www.nohmask21.com

There are two types of traditional drum used in Japan, the hourglass-shaped *tsuzumi*, and *taiko*. The *tsuzumi* has a lacquered wood body covered at each end with horsehide. The skins are laced to the body using string. A performer beats the drum with their right hand while tightening or loosening the strings with their left hand to produce different sounds.

The two most common types of *taiko* drum are the *shimedaiko* and *donagadaiko*. Both of which use cowhide and are played by striking them with sticks. The *shimedaiko* looks like a snare drum and produces a high-pitched, light, dry sound. The *donagadaiko* looks like a barrel and the biggest are about two meters long. They have a deep, loud sound and are sometimes played by two players.

日本には2種類の伝統的な太鼓があります。砂時計の形をした鼓と、太鼓です。鼓は漆塗りが施された胴の両側に馬の皮を張ってあります。皮はひもで結わえつけられています。奏者は右手で鼓を打ちながら左手でひもを締めたり緩めたりして音を変えます。

最もよく知られている太鼓には締太鼓と胴長太鼓の2種類があります。どちらも牛の皮を張ってあり、ばちを使って演奏します。締太鼓はスネアドラムに似ていてかん高く、軽快で乾いた音がします。胴長太鼓は樽のような形をしていて大きなものは2メートルにもなります。深く大きな音がして2人で演奏することもあります。

WAKA 和歌

キーワード	
verse	韻文
syllable	音節/文字
line	行
noble family	公家/貴族
exclusively	もっぱら
commoner	庶民
be based on	〜に基づいている
over time	やがて
dominant	優勢な
synonymous with	〜と同じ意味の

Waka is a style of verse usually containing thirty-one syllables in five lines. It follows a 5-7-5-7-7 syllable pattern. *Waka* is probably the oldest poetic style in Japan. In the Heian period (784-1185) the exchange of romantic *waka* between men and women of noble families became popular. However, *waka* was used almost exclusively by the nobles, and was never very popular among commoners. In the past there were several styles of *waka*. They were all based on a similar syllable pattern, but had different lengths. Over time, however, the five-line style known as *tanka* became dominant and is the only style still popular today. Indeed, the term *tanka* has now become synonymous with *waka*.

和歌は韻文の一種で5行31文字で表されます。5-7-5-7-7の形式です。和歌はおそらく日本で1番古い形の詩と考えられています。平安時代(784年〜1185年)には公家の男女の間でロマンティックな和歌のやり取りが流行しました。しかし一方で公家の間にしか広まらず庶民にはあまり縁のないものでした。昔は数種類の和歌がありました。そのどれもが似たような音節の形式に基づいて作られていて、長さだけが違っていました。やがて短歌として知られていた5行の形の和歌が優勢になり、今ではよく知られている詩形はこれだけになっています。和歌と言えば今では短歌のことを指します。

HYAKUNIN ISSHU | 百人一首

キーワード	
come to	〜するようになる
portrait	肖像
spread out	広げる

This is a collection of one hundred *waka* written by one hundred different poets between the seventh and thirteenth centuries. Eventually, they came to be used for a popular card game. This game uses two sets of one hundred cards each. One set has *waka* printed on one side with a portrait of each poet. On the second set only the last fourteen syllables of each *waka* are printed. This second set is spread out on the floor. One player, the reader, holds up a card from the first set and begins reading the poem. The other players must find the matching card from the cards on the floor.

これは7世紀から13世紀にかけて100人の歌人によって書かれた和歌を100首集めたものです。やがて人気のあるかるた遊びとして使われるようになりました。この遊びでは100枚の札を2組使います。1組には和歌とその作者の肖像が描かれています。もう1組には和歌の最後の14文字のみが書かれていて、これは床の上に並べられます。読み手は絵がついた方の札を持ち、そこに書いてある和歌を読みます。取り手は並べた札の中から正しい札を探します。

HAIKU/SENRYU 俳句/川柳

キーワード

indicating	表す
contribution	投稿
reaction	受け止め方/反応
object	もの/対象
encounter	思いがけなく出会う
ancient	古びた
pond	池
frog	かえる
splash	ぽちゃんと音をたてて飛び込む
journey	旅
interrupted by	〜で中断された
sickness	病気
withered	枯れた
amateur	素人

Haiku and *senryu* are forms of poetry. They each have seventeen syllables in three lines in a 5-7-5 pattern. Haiku contain words indicating the season (*kigo*). *Haijin* (haiku poets) often have pen names called *haigo*. One of the greatest *haijin* was Matsuo Basho who wrote many haiku while traveling. Many people still enjoy reading and writing haiku today, and newspapers often have columns full of haiku contributions.

Senryu has the same form as haiku, but a different focus. Haiku is traditionally about the poet's reaction to objects they encounter. *Senryu*, on the other hand, is about daily life and is often comical.

俳句も川柳も詩の一種です。どちらも5-7-5の形式、3行17文字で作られます。俳句には季節を表す言葉（季語）が含まれています。俳人（俳句の詩人）には俳号と呼ばれるペンネームがあります。最も偉大な俳人の1人は松尾芭蕉で、彼は旅をしながらたくさんの俳句を詠みました。現在でも多くの人が俳句を鑑賞したり詠んだりして楽しんでいます。新聞には投稿された俳句をたくさん掲載してある欄もよくあります。

川柳は俳句と同じ形式ですが、視点が違います。俳句は詩人が思いがけなく出会ったものに対する受け止め方を表現するものです。一方の川柳は日常生活について詠むことが多く、たいていは滑稽です。

- The poem "Furuikeya kawazutobikomu mizunooto" (By the ancient pond, a frog splashes in, the sound of water) by Basho is very famous. *Kawazu* (frog) is a Spring *kigo*.
  芭蕉の「古池や蛙飛び込む水の音」という俳句は非常に有名です。蛙は春の季語です。
- The poem "Tabiniyande yumewakarenoo kakemeguru" (My journey interrupted by sickness, only my dreams can travel the withered landscape) was the last poem Basho wrote before he died.
  「旅に病んで夢は枯れ野をかけめぐる」は芭蕉の辞世の句です。
- Some companies or groups hold *senryu* competitions for amateur poets.
  一般の人から応募された川柳のコンテストを行っている企業や団体もあります。

IGO | 囲碁

キーワード

grid 格子/碁盤目
vertical 縦の
horizontal 横の
take turns 交互に〜をする
place 置く
unoccupied
空いている/占領されていない
intersection （碁盤の）目/交点
besiege 包囲する
capture 捕らえる
surround ~ with . . .
〜を...で囲む

Also known as go, igo is a game played on a grid of nineteen vertical and nineteen horizontal lines. Two players, one with white stones and the other with black, take turns placing their stones on unoccupied intersections of the grid. Their goal is to control as much of the board as possible. The Chinese character for *i* means to besiege. Players can capture their opponent's pieces by surrounding them with their own. Players can basically place their stones on any unoccupied intersection; there are very few rules.

碁とも呼ばれる囲碁は縦横19本の線でできた格子を使って遊ぶゲームです。対局者はそれぞれが白い石と黒い石を持ち、空いている目に交互に石を打っていきます。碁盤をできるだけ多く占領することで勝敗が決まります。囲という漢字は包囲する、という意味です。対局者は相手の石を自分の石で囲むことによって捕らえることができます。空いている場所であればどこに石を打っても良いことになっています。決まり事はそう多くはありません。

SHOGI | 将棋

キーワード	
promote	成らせる（昇進させる）
territory	陣地
pawn	ポーン（チェスの駒の1つ）

Shogi, sometimes called Japanese chess, is played on a board with eighty-one squares. Each player has twenty flat, wooden pieces of eight different types. The name of each piece is written on its top. As in chess, the objective of the game is to capture your opponent's king (*osho*). There are, however, two major differences between *shogi* and chess. One difference is that captured pieces can be used by your opponent, and the other is that most pieces can be promoted when they reach the back of your opponents territory (like pawns in chess).

将棋は日本のチェスとも呼ばれ、81マスの盤面を使って遊びます。対局者はそれぞれ8種類20個の平らな木製の駒を使います。駒の名前はそれぞれの表面に書かれています。チェスのように相手の王（王将）を詰めると勝敗が決まります。しかし将棋とチェスでは大きく違う点が2つあります。1つは捕えられた持ち駒は相手に使われてしまうということ、もう1つは持ち駒が相手の陣地の奥に入ると、そのほとんどが（チェスのポーンのように）成る（昇格する）ということです。

SHIRO 城

キーワード	
be divided into	～に分けられる
province	領土/地方
lord	領主
territory	領土
show off	誇示する
residence	住居
military base	軍事拠点
defensive	防御用の
device	仕掛け
moat	堀
the Imperial Palace	皇居
preserve	保存する
plateau	台地
slope	斜面
steepen	急勾配にする
maze	迷路
confuse	混乱させる
magnificent	壮大な
immediate servant	直属の家臣
stand on	～に建つ
foundation	土台
own	所有する
mythical	神話の/想像上の
creature	生き物
be mounted	設置される
on the roof of	～の屋根の上に
be burnt down	焼失する
feudal lord	領主

Long ago Japan was divided into many small provinces. The lords of each province fought to take each other's territory. Castles were built by the lords to show off their power and to control their provinces. They were both residences and military bases. They were made of wood, but used various defensive devices for protection. For example, moats were built around some castles. In fact, the moats around the Imperial Palace in Tokyo, which used to be Edo Castle, are still preserved. Additionally, many castles were built on plateaus or hills. The slopes were then steepened, making them difficult for enemies to climb. In some castles the grounds from the gate to the main building were designed like a maze to confuse enemies. The main castle building is usually in the center and is called the *tensyukaku*. They are tall and magnificent structures. The lords and their immediate servants lived in the *tensyukaku*.

昔の日本はいくつもの小さな領土に分かれていました。それぞれの領主はお互いの領土を奪うために戦いました。城は領主が自分たちの権力を誇示し、領土を支配するために造られました。城は住居であり軍事拠点でもありました。木造建築ですが、防御のためのさまざまな仕掛けが凝らされていました。例えば周りに堀がめぐらされた城もありました。事実、東京の皇居周辺にある堀は江戸城のもので、今も保存されています。高台や丘の上に建てられた城も多くあります。斜面を急角度にして敵が登りにくいようにしてありました。敵を混乱させるため、門から中心となる建物までの道が迷路のように設計されている城もあります。中心となる建物はたいてい中央にあり、天守閣と呼ばれます。高く壮大な建物です。ここには領主と直属の家臣が住んでいました。

Himeji Castle 写真提供:姫路市

Himeji Castle 写真提供：姫路市

- Himeji Castle in Hyogo has the biggest *tenshukaku* in Japan. It's about thirty-one meters high and stands on a fifteen-meter foundation.
  兵庫の姫路城は日本で最も大きな天守閣があります。約31メートルの高さの建物が約15メートルの石垣の上に建てられています。
- Inuyama Castle in Aichi is the oldest existing castle in Japan. It was owned by a family until 2004.
  愛知の犬山城は現存する日本最古のお城で、2004年までは個人が所有していました。
- *Shachi*, mythical creatures with the head of an animal and the body of a fish, are mounted on the roof of the *tenshukaku*.
  天守閣の屋根にはしゃちと呼ばれる頭部は獣、体は魚の形をした想像上の生き物の置物が載せられています。
- The *tenshukaku* at Edo Castle, where the shogun lived in the Edo period (1603-1867), was about sixty meters high and the biggest building in Japan until it was burnt down.
  江戸時代（1603年〜1867年）の将軍が住んでいた江戸城の天守閣は高さが約60メートルあり、焼失するまでは日本最大の建築物でした。
- Many Japanese feudal lords had houses around Edo Castle, and we can still see some of their gardens around the Imperial Palace today.
  江戸城の周りには大名屋敷がたくさん建てられていました。今でも皇居周辺に当時の庭園を見ることができます。

JIIN | 寺院

キーワード

architecture	建築様式
statue	彫像
Statues of Buddha	仏像
place	置く
attract	惹きつける
the wealthy	裕福な人々
ensure	確かにする
prosperity	繁栄
leading statesman	政治家のトップ/有力な政治家
cabinet	飾り棚
display	安置する
as a sign of	～のしるしとして
faith	信仰心
ancestor	先祖
belong to	～に属する
particular	特定の
rely on	～を頼りにする
religious service	宗教的な行事
funeral	葬式
in exchange for	～の代わりに
donation	寄付/お布施
New Year's Day	正月/元日
monk	僧
nun	尼僧
sect	宗派
shave one's head	髪をそる

Temples are known for their beautiful architecture, statues and gardens. Statues of Buddha are placed in temples. There are many famous old temples all over Japan that attract large numbers of visitors. Some temples were built by the wealthy to ensure prosperity for the family. One of the most famous is Horyuji temple in Nara, which was built by Shotoku Taishi, a leading statesman of the Asuka period (593-710). Today many people have a small cabinet containing an image of Buddha called a *butsudan* in their homes. It is displayed as a sign of their faith and respect for their ancestors.

お寺はその美しい建築様式、彫像、庭園などで知られています。お寺には仏像が安置されています。日本各地にいくつもの有名な古いお寺があり、多くの観光客を惹きつけています。裕福な人たちが一族の繁栄を確かにするために建立したお寺もありました。最も有名なものの1つが奈良にある法隆寺で、これは飛鳥時代(593年～710年)の政治家のトップ、聖徳太子によって建立されました。現在では多くの家庭に仏壇と呼ばれる仏陀の影像や肖像が置かれた小さな飾り棚のようなものがあります。これは信仰心と、先祖を敬うしるしとして安置されています。

- *Danka* are groups of families which belong to a particular Buddhist temple. They rely on this temple for religious services like funerals, in exchange for donations.
  檀家は特定のお寺に属する家の集まりです。檀家はこのお寺に葬儀などの宗教行事を依頼して、代わりにお布施を渡します。
- Some people visit temples on New Year's Day to pray for health and happiness.
  お正月には健康や幸せを祈願しにお寺に行く人もいます。
- Monks and nuns of certain Buddhist sects shave their heads.
  僧侶は宗派によっては髪をそることもあります。
- Monks usually wear black kimono.
  僧侶はたいていは黒い着物を着ています。

JINJA | 神社

キーワード

represent	象徴する
religion	宗教
unique to	〜に特有の
basic premise	基本前提
household altar	神棚
special occasion	特別な日
entrance	入口
stone statue	石像
guard	守る
Shinto priest	神主
construct	建設する
bow	礼拝する
slightly	軽く
deeply	深く
clap	拍手する

There are over eighty thousand Shinto shrines in Japan, and they represent the oldest architectural style in the country. Shinto is a religion unique to Japan. Respect for the land and nature is its basic premise. Usually there is a mirror in a case inside each shrine. This is the symbol of the shrine's god. Shinto customs are common in Japanese life. Some people have household altars and pray for good health, success and happiness every day. However, most Japanese visit shrines only on special occasions.

日本には8万を超える神社があり、日本の最も古い建築様式を象徴しています。神道は日本特有の宗教で、土地や自然を敬うということが基本前提となっています。通常、神社には箱に収められた鏡が置かれています。これは神社の神の象徴とされています。神道を信仰することは日本人の生活に根ざしています。家に神棚を祀って健康、繁栄、幸福を毎日祈っている人もいます。しかし日本人の多くは特別な日にしか神社にお参りしません。

- The entrance to a shrine is marked by a huge gate called a *torii*. These are usually made of wood or stone, some painted bright red. Some shrines have two or three *torii*.
  神社の入口は鳥居と呼ばれる大きな門が特徴的です。たいていは木製か石造りで、鮮やかな赤に塗られているものもあります。鳥居が2つ、3つある神社もあります。
- A pair of stone statues called *komainu* guard the entrance to the shrine and its buildings. They are mythical creatures. One's mouth is usually open while the other's is closed.
  狛犬と呼ばれる石像が一対、神社の入口や建物の前を守っています。これは想像上の生き物です。たいていは片方が口を開け、もう片方は閉じています。
- A Shinto priest wears a kimono, *hakama* (see page 60) and one of two hats called *eboshi* and *kanmuri*.
  神主は着物を着て袴をはき、烏帽子か冠と呼ばれる2つの帽子のうちのどちらかをかぶっています。
- A *miko* is a woman who helps the priest. She wears a white kimono and red *hakama*.
  巫女は神主の手伝いをする女性です。白い着物に赤い袴をはいています。
- When a new building is constructed, a priest is asked to pray to the god of the land.
  新しく建物を建てる時には神主を呼んで、土地の神様にお祈りしてもらいます。
- How to pray at a shrine:
  After washing your hands and rinsing your mouth with water at the entrance, walk up to the shrine and bow slightly. Ring the bell and make a donation at the *saisenbako* (the donation box). Then bow twice deeply, clap twice and bow once deeply.
  参拝の作法:
  入口の水で手や口を清め、社殿に向かい、浅く礼拝します。鈴を鳴らしてから賽銭箱に賽銭を入れます。それから2回深く礼拝をして2回手を打ち、もう1回深く礼拝します。

JAPANESE GARDENS | 日本庭園

キーワード	
attempt to	～を試みる
recreate	再現する
landform	地形
creek	小川
civil war	内乱/戦国時代
pebble	小石
abstract representation	抽象的な表現
luxurious	豪華な

The Japanese have been making beautiful gardens for over a thousand years. There have been many different styles throughout history, but they all attempt to recreate natural landforms. The first gardens often had creeks or ponds, sometimes with an island. During the Muromachi period (1336-1573) the *karesansui* style was born. This new style was very popular during Japan's long period of civil war (fifteenth to sixteenth century). It used rocks, stones and pebbles to create very abstract representations of nature. For example, a large rock in a bed of white sand might represent an island in the sea. The most famous of these gardens is in Ryoanji temple in Kyoto. Later, teahouses were built in many gardens and a *chaniwa* (a gray stone path) leading to the teahouse was added. During the Edo period (1603-1867), feudal lords built huge gardens with ponds, miniature mountains, rocks, bridges and teahouses. These luxurious gardens contained many plants and trees. Gardens of this style are still common in Japan today, and the three most famous are Korakuen, Kairakuen, and Kenrokuen.

日本人は千年以上も前から美しい庭園を造ってきました。歴史上いろいろな様式の庭園がありますが、そのどれもが自然の地形を再現しようとしています。初期の庭園には小川や池があり、池には島が造られていることもありました。室町時代（1336年～1573年）には枯山水様式が生まれました。この様式は日本の長い戦国時代（15世紀から16世紀）の間に大変流行しました。岩や石、小石を使って自然の抽象的な表現を造りだそうとしました。例えば白い砂を広く敷き詰めた中に置いた大きな岩は海に浮かんだ島を表しています。この様式の庭園で最も有名なものは京都の竜安寺です。後には多くの庭園に茶室が造られ、また茶室に向かう茶庭（灰色の石の小道）もつけ足されました。江戸時代（1603年～1867年）には大名が池やミニチュアの山、岩、橋、茶室などを配置した巨大な庭園を築きました。これら豪華な庭園には植物や樹木もたくさん植えられていました。この様式の庭園は現在の日本でもよく知られていて、有名三大庭園は後楽園、偕楽園、兼六園です。

53

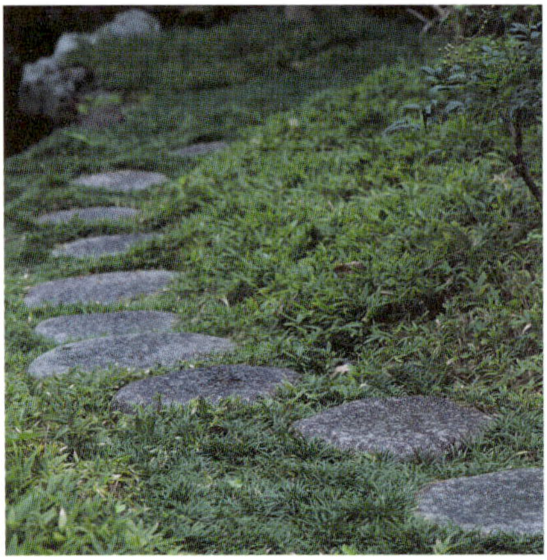
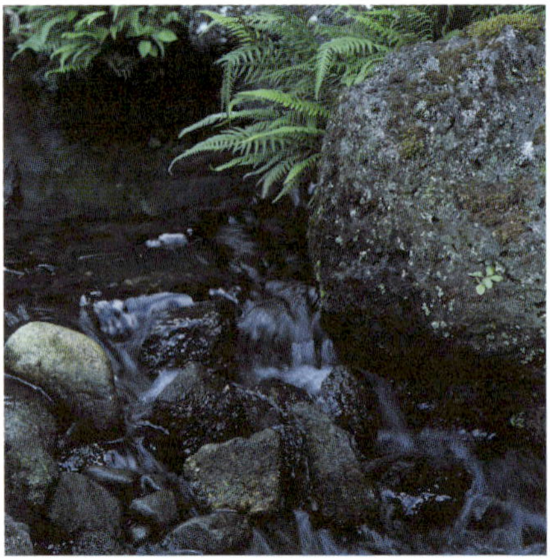
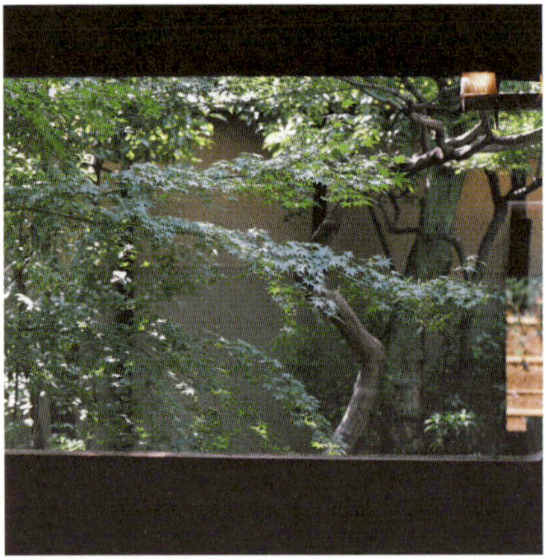
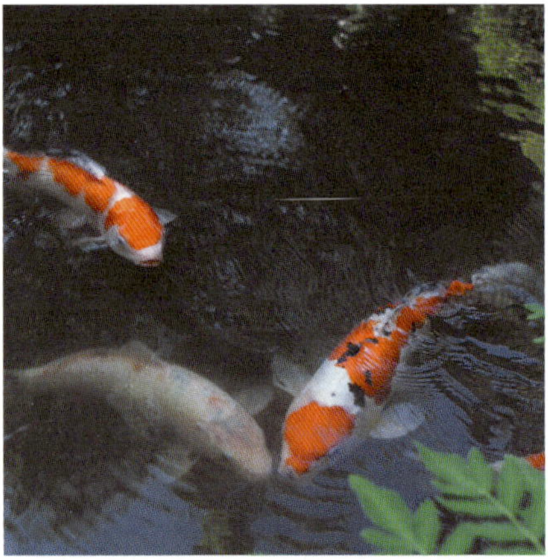
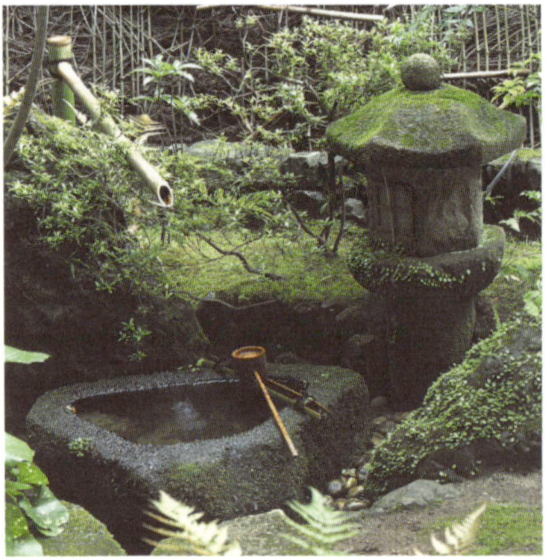
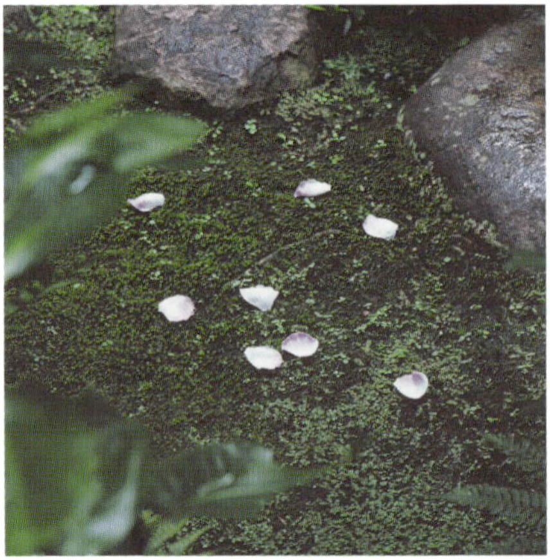

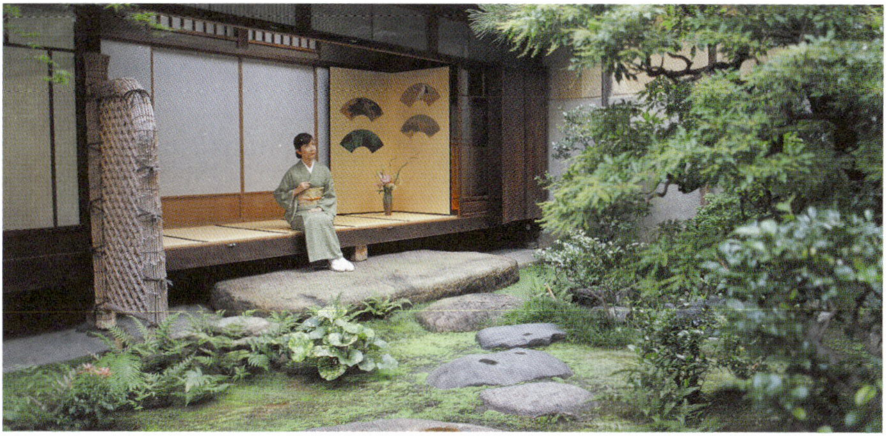

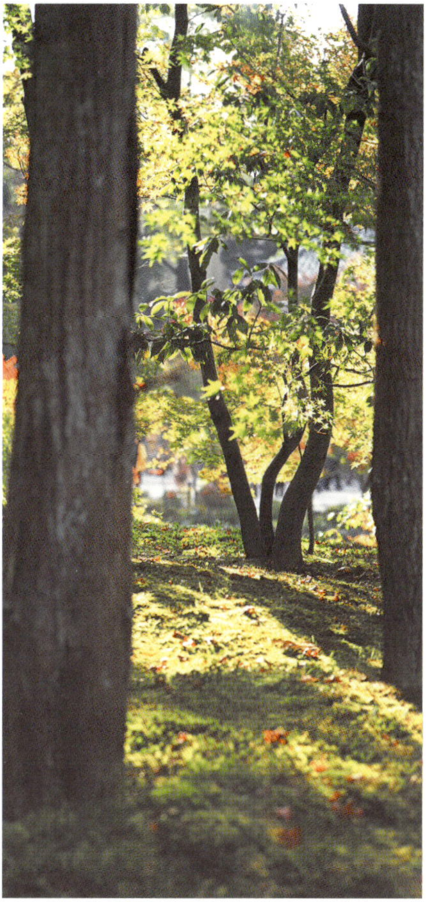

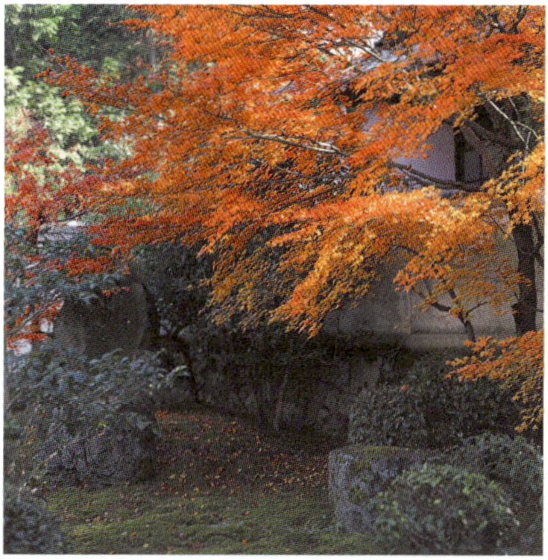

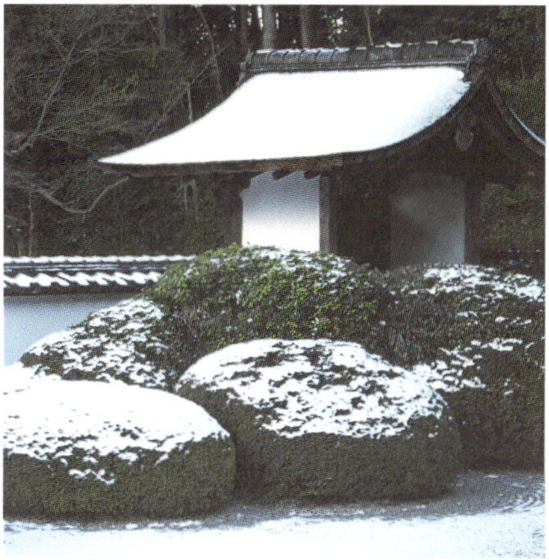

TRADITIONAL ARCHITECTURE | 伝統建築

キーワード

material of choice	最高の素材
be good for	～に効く/～に効果がある
resist earthquake	地震に耐える
breathe	通気性がある
clay	粘土
roofing	屋根ふき
durable	耐久力のある
raised wooden floor	木製の高床
allow for	～の効果がある
airflow	空気の流れ/風通し
sheaf	束
compressed	圧縮した
woven rushes	織ったいぐさ
be hemmed with	縁を～で縫う
trap	閉じ込める
be partitioned by	～で間仕切りされる
divider	仕切
wooden frame	木枠
entryway	入口
surrounded by	～で取り囲まれた
national treasure	国宝
grid frame	格子枠
primarily	主に
glass	ガラス

Wood was the material of choice for traditional Japanese buildings, as it is very good for resisting earthquakes and breathes well in the hot summers.

Kawara (baked clay tiles) were sometimes used for roofing, but usually only at temples or shrines, as they were quite expensive. *Kawara* are very durable and some buildings still have tiles from their original construction hundreds of years ago.

Most buildings had raised wooden floors, which allowed for greater airflow during the hot summers. Tatami mats are typically square and measure about a hundred and eighty by ninety centimeters. They are made from sheaves of rice straw compressed from about forty centimeters thickness down to about five or six centimeters thickness. The compressed straw is then covered with woven rushes and hemmed with beautiful cloth. Tatami mats trap air, helping rooms to stay cool in summer and warm in winter.

日本の伝統建築には、耐震性があり暑い夏でも風通しの良い材木が最高の素材でした。

瓦（粘土を焼いて作ったタイル）は屋根のふき材に使われることもありましたが、大変高価でしたので寺院や神社にしか使われていませんでした。瓦は大変耐久性に優れているので、建物によっては何百年も前に建てられた当時のままの瓦が残っていることもあります。

ほとんどの建物の床は、木製で高めに作られていたので夏の暑い間は風通しを良くする効果がありました。典型的な畳は四角く、180×90センチの大きさです。40センチほどの厚みに積んだわらを5、6センチの厚みになるまで圧縮して作ります。織ったいぐさで作った畳表で圧縮したわらを覆い、美しい布で縁を縫います。畳は空気を閉じ込めるので、夏は部屋を涼しく冬は暖かくするのに役立ちます。

be mounted on rails	敷居にはめる
fragile	破れやすい
mobile	可動性の
be folded into	～に折られる
export	輸出する
overseas	海外に
be supported by	～に支えられている
all but	ほとんど
disappear from	～から消える
support post	支柱
breadwinner	一家の稼ぎ手
step on	～を踏む
edge	縁
be measured by	～で示す/～で測られる
the number of	～の数
tongue twister	早口言葉
beautifully	美しく

Houses often contained just one big room, and these rooms were partitioned by various types of dividers. *Fusuma*, wooden frames holding beautifully painted paper or silk sheets, were used as walls or entryways. Some castles and temples had rooms surrounded by *fusuma* with beautiful, colorful paint or ink pictures. Many of these *fusuma* are now national treasures.

Shoji are similar to *fusuma*, but have a grid frame, and are used primarily as windows or doors. Their paper sections allow a soft light to shine through into the room, and they have remained popular even with the introduction of glass. Both *shoji* and *fusuma* are mounted on rails and can be slid opened and closed. The fragile paper sections are often damaged, but can be easily repaired.

1軒の家には大きな部屋が1部屋しかないことが多く、いろいろな種類の仕切で間仕切りされていました。襖は木製の枠に美しく絵を描いた紙や絹を貼ったもので、壁や入口として使われていました。美しい色彩や墨で絵が描かれた襖に囲まれた部屋のある城や寺院もあります。これらの襖の多くは現在では国宝になっています。

障子は襖と似ていますが枠が格子になっていて、主に窓やドアとして使われています。紙の部分からは柔らかい日の光が差し込み、ガラスが伝来してからも使われ続けています。障子も襖も敷居にはめてスライドさせ、開け閉めします。紙の部分は破れやすいのですが、簡単に貼り替えることができます。

Byobu were mobile partitions or blinds. They could be folded into two, four or six sections and, like *fusuma*, had painted paper coverings. *Byobu* became quite popular around the world and many were exported to overseas art collectors during the fifteenth and sixteenth centuries.

Tsuitate were similar to *byobu*, but were supported by stands and could not be folded into sections. Although *fusuma* and *shoji* are still often seen today, *byobu* and *tsuitate* have all but disappeared from Japanese homes.

屏風は持ち運びできる仕切またはブラインドでした。2つ折り、4つ折り、6つ折りなどにでき、襖のように絵が描かれた紙が貼ってありました。屏風は世界中に広まり、15世紀から16世紀にかけては海外の美術収集家に向けて輸出されていました。

ついたては屏風と似ていますが、台に支えられていて折り畳むことはできません。

襖や障子は今日でもよく目にすることがありますが、屏風やついたては日本の住宅からほとんど消えてしまいました。

- The *daikoku-bashira* is the main support post of a house, but the word also means breadwinner.
  大黒柱は家屋の中心にある支柱のことですが、一家の稼ぎ手という意味で使われることもあります。
- We sometimes use a carpet woven from rushes in summer.
  夏の間、いぐさでできたラグのようなものを床に敷くこともあります。
- It's bad manners to step on the edges of a tatami mat.
  畳の縁を踏むことは不作法なこととされています。
- The size of a Japanese room is measured by the number of tatami mats needed to cover the floor.
  和室の広さは床を覆う畳の数で表します。
- "Bozuga byobuni jozuni bozuno eokaita" is a Japanese tongue twister. (A monk painted a monk on a *byobu* beautifully.)
  早口言葉に「坊主が屏風に上手に坊主の絵を描いた」というものがあります。

KIMONO 着物

キーワード

refer to	〜を指す
clothing	衣類
lead to	結局〜となる
distinction	区別
frequently	よく/頻繁に
formal occasion	フォーマルな機会
garment	衣服
undergarment	下着
collar	襟
sash	飾り帯
decorative	装飾的な
toe	足指
thong	ひも
Coming of Age Day	成人の日
plain	無地の
expensive	高価な
care for / look after	手入れをする/管理する
rent	レンタルする
special occasions	特別な機会
put on	身につける
beauty salon	美容院
offer	提供する

Although the word kimono is now used to refer to the elegant, traditional dress of Japanese women and men, it originally meant clothes. It referred to any type of clothing worn in Japan. This changed after the introduction of Western culture to Japan, which led to the distinction between *yofuku*, Western clothes, and *wafuku* or kimono, Japanese clothes. Slowly, Western styles became more and more popular for everyday life, and Japanese clothes were only worn in formal situations. Since then, the word kimono has been used to refer only to formal Japanese clothes. These days kimono are worn frequently only by people working in certain service industries such as hotels or restaurants. They are also worn for very formal occasions such as weddings.

着物という言葉は現在、日本人の男女が身につける上品で伝統的な正装という意味で使われますが、元々は着る物という意味です。どんなものであれ、衣類は全て着物と呼ばれていました。この呼び方は日本に西洋の文化が紹介されてから変わりました。西洋の衣服を洋服と呼び、日本の衣服を和服、または着物と呼んで区別するようになったのです。洋服は徐々に日常生活に浸透していき、着物はフォーマルな場でしか着られなくなりました。こうして着物という言葉は日本の正装という意味で使われるようになったのです。現在では着物を頻繁に着るのはホテルやレストランといった特定のサービス業の従業員だけになっています。また結婚式など非常にフォーマルな場でも着ることがあります。

In addition to the main garment, the standard kimono has several parts to it: a full length undergarment called a *nagajuban*, a collar accessory called a *han-eri*, a sash called an obi, a decorative string called an *obijime*, and *tabi*, which are short, white socks that separate the big toe from the other toes. *Zori* or *geta* are the footwear traditionally worn with a kimono. *Zori*, usually worn on more formal occasions, look like sandals and have thongs of leather or beautifully patterned cloth. *Geta*, worn in more casual situations, are also like wood sandals, but are raised on two short wooden supports.

一般的にメインの着物以外に付属品がいくつかあります。長襦袢という長い下着と半襟という襟の飾り、帯というサッシュ、帯締めという飾りひも、そして足袋という親指と他の指が分かれている短い白のソックスです。着物を着た時の履物は草履や下駄です。草履はより正式な場で履くサンダルのようなもので、革や美しい模様の布でできた鼻緒がついています。下駄はよりカジュアルな履物で、やはり木製のサンダルに似ていますが、底に短い木製の歯が2つついています。

There are several types of kimono, each worn in different situations. *Furisode* are for single women and have very long sleeves that almost reach the ground. They are usually worn for Coming of Age Day (see page 126). *Kurotomesode* are typically black with a pattern at the bottom and are worn by married women. A plain black kimono is worn for funerals. There are also casual kimono, and light kimono for summer called *yukata*. Kimono are usually made of expensive silk, but *yukata* are made of cotton, which is cheaper and easier to care for. In fact, *yukata* were originally used as bathrobes. Men also wear a type of kimono called *haorihakama*. The *haori* is a type of kimono jacket, while the *hakama* are a pair of loose fitting pants. Married and single men both wear *haorihakama*.

着物にはいくつかの種類があり、それぞれ違った用途で着ます。振袖は未婚の女性用で地面に届きそうな長い袖がついています。これは成人の日によく着られます。黒留袖は既婚の女性用で黒い着物の裾に模様がついています。無地の黒い着物は葬式用です。またカジュアルな着物や、浴衣と呼ばれる夏用の簡素な着物もあります。着物はたいていは高価な絹で作られていますが、浴衣は木綿で作られているので安く、手入れも簡単です。実際浴衣はバスローブとして使われていました。男性は羽織袴と呼ばれる着物を着ます。羽織は上着のようなもので、袴はゆったりしたズボンのようなものです。男性は未婚でも既婚でも羽織袴を着ます。

Furisode

Kurotomesode

- The image of a kimono can be changed simply by changing accessories.
  着物は合わせる小物でいろいろな違ったイメージになります。
- Kimono are very expensive and difficult to look after so some people rent them for special occasions.
  着物はとても高価で手入れも難しいので必要な時にだけレンタルする人もいます。
- Kimono are difficult to put on, so many beauty salons offer hair, make-up and dressing services to create the traditional Japanese look.
  着付けは難しいので、髪のセットやメイク、着付けをしてくれる美容院がたくさんあります。

CHINA 陶器

キーワード	
meal	食事
serve	（食事などを）出す
dish	料理
vessel	容器
platter	大皿
pottery producing region	陶器の産地
have an influence on	～に影響を与える
significant	重要な

Meals in Japan are not usually served on one large plate as they are in the West. Instead, each dish is served in its own vessel. Therefore, families typically use a lot of china. They need bowls, plates, cups, and platters of various shapes and sizes. There are also formal teacups for guests. Arita is one of Japan's most famous pottery producing regions and in the seventeenth century, its techniques had a significant influence on European porcelain.

日本の食事は欧米のように1枚の大きな皿に盛り付けて出しません。料理によって違った器に盛り付けられます。このため家庭では食器をたくさん使います。いろいろな形や大きさの鉢・椀、皿、カップ、大皿が必要です。お客様用のフォーマルな茶碗もあります。有田は日本有数の陶器の産地で、17世紀にはその技術はヨーロッパの磁器に大きな影響を与えました。

LACQUERWARE 漆器

キーワード	
sap	樹液
varnish tree	漆の木
chopsticks	箸
lacquering technique	漆塗りの技術
at that time	その頃
craftsman	職人

Lacquerware is produced by coating wood with the sap of the varnish tree. It's used for making soup bowls, lunch boxes, chopsticks, and many other products. Some of the most beautiful lacquerware art is used for temple and shrine decorations. Japanese lacquering techniques improved greatly in the sixth century. At that time, craftsmen started adding patterns of gold and silver to their products.

漆器は材木に漆の木の樹液を塗って作ります。汁椀、弁当箱、箸などいろいろな製品に使われています。最も素晴らしい漆塗りの技法のいくつかが寺院や神社の装飾に使われています。日本の漆塗りの技術は6世紀に大いに向上しました。その頃に工芸職人が製品に金・銀を使った模様を入れ始めました。

CHOPSTICKS 箸

キーワード	
bamboo	竹
disposable	使い捨てにできる
be given out free	
無料で配られる	
wave ~ over . . .	
…の上で~を振る	
decide	決める
stick ~ into . . .	
~を…に刺す	
examine	探る/調べる
lick	なめる
drag	引きずる
towards	~の方へ

Japanese chopsticks are made of wood, bamboo or plastic. They are shorter and lighter than Chinese chopsticks. Each family member has his or her own set. Disposable wooden chopsticks are used at restaurants, and are given out free with food bought at takeout shops. A lot of people bring homemade lunches to work or school with their own set in a chopstick case. Children start to practice using chopsticks when they are around three. Until then they use forks or spoons.

日本の箸は木、竹、プラスティックなどでできています。中国の箸よりも短く、軽いです。家族全員が自分専用の箸を持っています。レストランでは使い捨ての木製の箸が使われ、テイクアウトの店では食べ物を買うと無料で箸がもらえます。仕事場や学校に手作りの弁当を持って来る人はたくさんいますが、この人たちは専用の箸箱に箸を入れて持って来ます。子どもは3才くらいから箸の使い方を練習し始めます。それまではフォークやスプーンを使います。

Bad Manners　マナー違反

- *Mayoi-bashi*: Don't wave your chopsticks over the food when deciding what to eat next.
  迷い箸：次にどの料理を食べるか決める時、食べ物の上で箸をあちこち動かさない。
- *Sashi-bashi*: Don't stick your chopsticks into the food.
  刺し箸：食べ物を箸で刺さない。
- *Saguri-bashi*: Don't use your chopsticks to examine food.
  探り箸：器の中の食べ物を箸で探らない。
- *Neburi-bashi*: Don't lick your chopsticks.
  ねぶり箸：箸をなめない。
- *Yose-bashi*: Don't use your chopsticks to drag bowls or plates towards you.
  寄せ箸：箸を使って食器を引き寄せない。

SADO 茶道

キーワード

establish 確立する
host 亭主（もてなす側）
prior to ～に先だって
a set of tea utensils 茶道具一式
provide しつらえる/準備する
pleasant atmosphere 心地良い雰囲気
strong （味が）濃い
bitter 苦い
in addition to ～に加えて
next to ～の隣に
support そえる
hold ~ above one's head ～を頭の上におしいただく
take a sip 一口飲む
make a slurping sound ズルズル音をたてる
wipe ぬぐう
away from ～から離れて
observe 鑑賞する

A man named Sen no Rikyu established *sado* (tea ceremony) as an art in the sixteenth century. Nowadays, it is a unique Japanese ritual. The host sits in a *chashitsu* (a room specially designed for tea ceremony), puts *maccha* (powdered green tea) in a teacup, mixes it and serves it to the guests. Prior to the ceremony, the host decorates the room with a *kakejiku* (hanging scroll) or a flower arrangement, prepares a set of tea utensils and provides a pleasant atmosphere for the guest. Both the host and the guests usually wear kimono. When the tea ceremony is held outdoors, it is called *nodate*. A red carpet is put in the yard, and tea is prepared for the guests. There are a number of tea ceremony styles and each teaches different techniques. Many junior and senior high schools and universities have tea ceremony clubs, and a tea ceremony is usually held at school festivals.

16世紀に千利休という男性が茶道を芸術として確立しました。今では日本独特の儀式となっています。亭主は茶室（茶道用にデザインされた部屋）に座り、茶碗に抹茶を入れ、混ぜ合わせ、客にふるまいます。また茶会に先がけて部屋を掛け軸やいけ花で飾り、茶道具一式を準備し、客にとって心地良い雰囲気をしつらえます。たいていは亭主も客も着物を着ます。屋外で催される茶会は野点と呼ばれます。庭に赤い敷物を敷いて、客にお茶をふるまいます。茶道の流派にはいくつかあり、それぞれが違った作法を教えています。中学校、高校、大学などでは茶道クラブがあるところも多く、学校祭で茶道が披露されることもあります。

- *Maccha* is very strong and bitter, so people usually eat sweets first and then drink the tea.
  抹茶はとても濃く苦いので、甘い和菓子を先にいただいてから飲みます。
- A formal tea ceremony takes about three hours and guests are offered meals in addition to tea.
  正式なお茶会は3時間ほどかかり、お茶とは別に食事も出されます。

Tea Manners

1. Place the teacup between you and the person sitting next to you. Say, "*Osaki ni.*" (Excuse me for going first.)
2. Then put the teacup in front of you and say, "*Otemae chodai shimasu*" (Thank you for the tea.) to the host and bow.
3. Put the teacup in the left hand and support it with your right hand. Hold it above your head in front of you.
4. Turn the teacup to the right twice and take a sip. Sip the tea until it is finished. One should make a slurping sound on the last sip.
5. Wipe the teacup with the thumb and index finger where your mouth touched it, and turn it to the left twice.
6. Then place the cup in front of you. Wipe your fingers with paper and place the teacup away from you towards the host.
7. Observe it while placing both hands on the tatami mat and put it back in its original position.

お茶のいただき方

1. 自分と隣りに座っている人の間に茶碗を置きます。「お先に」と言います。
2. 茶碗を自分の前に置き、「お点前頂戴します」と亭主に言い、お辞儀をします。
3. 左手に茶碗をのせ、右手をそえます。そして頭の上においしいただきます。
4. 右に2回茶碗を回し、一口飲みます。最後まで飲み干します。最後の一口は音をたててすすります。
5. 茶碗の口が触れたところを親指と人差し指でぬぐい、左に2回茶碗を回します。
6. 自分の前に茶碗を置きます。懐紙で指をぬぐい、自分から離して亭主の方向に茶碗を置きます。
7. 両手を畳について茶碗を鑑賞し、茶碗を元の位置に戻します。

IKEBANA | いけ花

キーワード

offering	お供え
recognized	認められた
significantly	はっきりと
depth	深さ
aim to	〜することを目指す
highlight	際だたせる
component	花材/構成材料
stem	茎
vine	つる
harmonious	調和のとれた
intend to	〜を意図する
shallow	浅い
container	容器
fix	固定する
in place	適当な位置に
required	必須の
vice versa	逆の場合も同じ
diploma	免状
title	肩書き
school	流派

It is thought that *ikebana* started with people bringing flower arrangements to Buddhist temples as offerings. As a recognized art form, however, Japanese flower arrangement began around five centuries ago and has since evolved into several different styles. It is similar to Western styles of flower arrangement in that there are seasonal influences, but there is significantly more depth of meaning to it than that. *Ikebana* aims to highlight the beauty of nature by arranging all components (flowers, stems, leaves, branches, vines, etc.) in a harmonious manner. While Western flower arrangements can be enjoyed from any angle, *ikebana* arrangements are intended to be viewed from just one. The vases used for *ikebana* are usually shallow containers or pots and the flowers are often fixed in place with metal needles.

いけ花は人々がお供えとして寺院に花を持って来たのが始まりとされています。しかしいけ花が芸術として認められるようになったのは500年ほど前からで、その後いろいろな流派に分かれていきました。季節の影響を受けるという点では欧米のフラワーアレンジメントに似ていますが、それよりもより深い意味がはっきりとあります。いけ花は調和のとれた作法で全ての花材（花、茎、葉、枝、つるなど）を生けることによって自然の美しさを際だたせることを目指しています。フラワーアレンジメントはどの角度から見ても楽しめますが、いけ花は一方向からのみ鑑賞できることを意図して生けられます。いけ花用の花器はたいていは浅い容器かつぼで、剣山を使って花を適当な位置に固定します。

- *Sado* and *ikebana* used to be required training before marriage. The training was not just about making good tea or arranging flowers but also to learn manners.
  茶道といけ花は花嫁修業の1つでした。花嫁修業はお茶を上手に入れたり、お花をきれいに生けたりする技術を身につけるためだけでなく礼儀作法を学ぶためのものでした。
- Many *sado* teachers also teach *ikebana* and vice versa.
  茶道の先生がいけ花を教えたり、またその逆もよくあります。
- After some time and training, one can receive a diploma and a title from their teacher.
  ある程度の稽古を積んだら先生から免状と肩書きをもらえます。
- There are many styles of *ikebana* but the Ikenobo school was the first.
  現在たくさんの流派がありますが、池坊流が宗家でした。

BONSAI 盆栽

キーワード
horticulture　園芸

shape　形を整える

growth　生長

trim　刈りそろえる

prune　刈り込む

force　無理やり行う

repot　別の鉢に植え替える

for decades　数十年の間

be passed down
（次の世代に）受け継がれる

Bonsai is part art and part horticulture. The most common bonsai are trees which produce flowers or berries at some point in the year, but trees which produce colorful autumn leaves are also used. Normally, a small tree is planted in a pot. The plant is allowed to grow, but the owner shapes it throughout its growth by trimming or pruning it. Sometimes, wires are used to force growth in a particular direction. As the bonsai gets larger, it may need to be repotted. Bonsai can live for decades or even centuries, and are often passed down from generation to generation within families.

盆栽は芸術であり園芸でもあります。よくある盆栽の木は1年のある時期に花や実をつける木ですが、秋に色づく木もよく使われます。普通は植木鉢に小さな木を植えます。植木は生長させても構いませんが、持ち主はその間中、剪定したり刈り込んだりして形を整えていきます。一定方向に育つように針金を使うこともあります。大きくなるにつれ植え替えが必要になることもあります。盆栽は何十年、ものによっては何世紀も生き続け、家族代々で受け継がれることもあります。

写真提供 上下とも： みやび園 島義典氏

SHOGUN | 将軍

キーワード

military government
軍事政権

nominate　任命する

reign　支配する

height of one's power
権力の絶頂

dissatisfied with
〜に不満を持った

cause 〜 to . . .
〜に...させる(原因となる)

strength　力

political power　政治権力

the Imperial Court　皇室

prohibit 〜 from . . .
〜が...することを禁止する

leaving　出ていくこと

entering　入って来ること

national isolation　鎖国

extreme　極端な

law　法律

hurt　傷つける

wild dog　のら犬

be put to death　死刑になる

successfully　うまく

reform　改革する

living quarters　住居空間

mistress　側室/愛人

The samurai military government started in Japan in about 1185. Minamoto no Yoritomo was nominated as the leader of Japan's government at that time. He was the first to be called shogun. After that, shogun and their samurai reigned throughout the Kamakura period (1185-1333), the Muromachi period (1336-1573) and the Edo period (1603-1867). It was during the Edo period that the shogun reached the height of their power. Shogun of this period are popular and their stories are often used as material for TV programs and movies today. Eventually, however, some samurai became dissatisfied with the shogun. This and the increasing influence of foreign powers caused the military government to lose strength. Finally in 1867, Tokugawa Yoshinobu, the fifteenth shogun of the Edo period, returned political power to the Imperial Court and the age of the shogun ended.

日本では1185年頃に侍による軍事政権が始まりました。源頼朝がその時代の日本政府の指導者に任命されました。彼は将軍と呼ばれた最初の人でした。その後の鎌倉時代(1185年〜1333年)、室町時代(1336年〜1573年)、江戸時代(1603年〜1867年)を通じて将軍と侍たちによる支配が続きました。江戸時代には将軍は権力の頂点に上り詰めました。この時代の将軍たちは人気があり、テレビ番組や映画の題材になることもよくあります。しかしそのうちに侍の中には将軍に対して不満を持つ者も現れました。このことや外国の影響力が増大したことにより軍事政権が力を失いました。ついに1867年に徳川15代将軍の慶喜は大政奉還をし、将軍の時代は終わりました。

- Tokugawa Iemitsu, the third shogun of the Edo period, prohibited people from leaving or entering Japan. This policy was called *sakoku* (national isolation).
  江戸時代の3代将軍徳川家光は、人々が海外に出かけたり、日本に入国したりすることを禁じました。これを「鎖国」と言います。
- Tokugawa Tsunayoshi, the fifth shogun of the Edo period, made extreme laws to protect animals. If, for example, people hurt a wild dog, they would be put to death.
  江戸時代の5代将軍徳川綱吉は極端な動物愛護の法律を作りました。例えばのら犬を傷つけると死刑になったりしました。
- Tokugawa Yoshimune, the eighth shogun of the Edo period, successfully reformed the government. There are many dramas and movies about him.
  江戸時代の8代将軍徳川吉宗は改革に取り組み、多くの功績を残しました。吉宗にちなんだドラマや映画もたくさん作られています。
- The living quarters of the shogun's mother, wife and mistresses was called the *ooku*. The shogun was the only man allowed to enter the *ooku*.
  将軍の母、正妻、側室の住居空間は大奥と呼ばれていました。大奥は将軍以外の男性は立ち入り禁止でした。

© PART ONE CO.,LTD. 1993

SAMURAI 侍

キーワード

devote oneself to
～に身を捧げる

knight　騎士

regional leader　地方の指導者

recruit　募る/新しく入れる

property　財産

academic　一般教養の

tradition　しきたり

worsen　さらに悪くなる

be forced to
～せざるを得ない

second job　内職/副業

code　ルール/礼儀作法

value　重んじる

trust　信(信頼)

honor　義(恩恵)

loyalty　忠(忠義)

serve　(人に)仕える

castle town　城下町

until one's death
～が死ぬまで

social status　社会的地位

lead a humble life
質素な生活を送る

masterless
(仕える)主人のいない

unemployed　仕事のない

fail　失敗する

intend to　～するつもりだ

following year　次の年

Samurai were warriors who devoted themselves to feudal lords. They were similar to European knights. They wore their hair in topknots and carried swords.

Samurai first appeared around the tenth century when regional leaders, recruited groups of men to protect their property. Over time academic study and the learning of martial arts became important parts of samurai tradition. In the middle of the Edo period (1603-1867), the economy worsened, and many samurai became poor. They were forced to seek second jobs such as making umbrellas. But they were still very proud of being samurai.

侍は領主に身を捧げた武士のことです。ヨーロッパの騎士によく似ていました。彼らはまげを結い、刀を差していました。

侍は10世紀頃、地方の指導者が自分の領地を守るために男性集団を募ったことに始まります。やがて学問や武術を身につけることが、侍のしきたりとして大切な部分になりました。江戸時代(1603年～1867年)の半ばに経済状況が悪化したため、侍の多くは生活が苦しくなりました。彼らは傘を作るといったような内職を探すことをせざる得なくなりました。しかし彼らはそれでもまだ侍であることを大変誇りに思っていました。

© PART ONE CO.,LTD. 1993

- *Bushido* is the Japanese warrior code. It valued trust, honor and loyalty.
  武士道は信・義・忠を重んじるという武士のルールを表したものです。
- Samurai usually served a lord and lived in a castle town. Once a samurai chose a lord, he usually served that lord until his death.
  侍はたいていどこかの領主に仕え、城下町に住んでいました。1度領主に仕えると一生奉公することが当たり前でした。
- During the Edo period, samurai had a high social status, but led humble lives.
  江戸時代、侍は高い身分にありましたが、生活は質素で苦しいものでした。
- Samurai who didn't serve a lord were called *ronin* (masterless samurai).
  領主に仕えない侍は浪人と呼ばれていました。
- Nowadays, unemployed students who fail their college or university entrance examinations, but intend to try again the following year, are called *ronin* students.
  今では大学受験に失敗し就職せずに、次の年もう1度トライする学生は浪人生と呼ばれています。

NINJA | 忍者

キーワード

contrary to	～に反して
literally	文字通り
invisible	隠れた
avoid	避ける
outfit	服装一式
blend in	うまく溶け込む
disguise oneself as	～の姿に変装する
street performer	大道芸人
rarely	めったに～ない
perform	行う
assassination	暗殺
tool	道具
weapon	武器
cling to	～に張りつく
ceiling	天井
secret codes	暗号
be tied into	～に編み込まれる
be sewn into	～に縫い込まれる
knowledge	知識
medicinal herb	薬草

Contrary to popular belief, ninja were basically just spies. They trained in the art of *ninjutsu*, literally the art of being invisible, and avoided fighting as much as possible. Although ninja occasionally wore the black outfits people usually imagine, most of the time they wore whatever was required to blend in. As they normally worked in towns or cities, they might have disguised themselves as anything from a street performer to a merchant. Their main objective was simply to gather information and only rarely did they perform assassinations. The two most famous ninja groups were the Koga ninja from Shiga, and the Iga ninja from Mie.

世間一般に信じられていることとは違って、忍者は実際はただのスパイです。彼らは忍術（文字通り隠れる術）を体得し、できるだけ戦いを避けました。時にはイメージ通りの黒い衣装を身につけていましたが、ほとんどの場合は、一般人にうまく溶け込むために必要な衣装ならば何でも着ていました。普段は町や都で活動していたので、大道芸人や商人のような扮装をしていたかもしれません。彼らの主な目的は情報を集めることで、人を殺すのはごく稀でした。とても有名な忍者の集団は滋賀の甲賀忍者と三重の伊賀忍者です。

- Ninja used many tools and weapons. One of the most popular is the *shuriken* (throwing star).
  忍者はいろいろな道具や武器を使っていました。とても有名なものの1つは手裏剣です。
- Ninja often planted quick growing plants in their gardens. They practiced jumping over these plants every day. As the plants got taller, the ninja learned to jump higher.
  忍者は生長の早い植物を庭に植えていました。毎日それを飛び越す訓練をしていました。植物が高く生長するにつれてより高く飛べるようになりました。
- Ninja did a lot of weight training so they would be strong enough to cling to walls and ceilings.
  忍者は壁や天井に張りつくことのできる力をつけるために、十分に体を鍛えていました。
- Important letters were written in secret codes and tied into a ninja's hair or sewn into their clothes.
  重要な書状は暗号で書かれ、髪の毛に編み込まれたり、服に縫い込まれたりしていました。
- Ninja had much knowledge about medicinal herbs.
  忍者は薬草についての知識も豊富にありました。

GEISHA 芸者

キーワード

essentially	本質的に
voluntary	自由意志で
prospective	見込みのある
dormitory	寮
routine	日課
fail to	〜できない
probationary	見習い中の
on-the-job training	実地研修
full geisha	一人前の芸者
mentor	助言者
exquisite	優美な

Geisha (Geigi in the Kansai area) are essentially entertainers at parties. Prior to World War II, girls from poor families were sold into geisha houses, but these days becoming a geisha is voluntary. Prospective geisha sign a contract with a geisha house, called an *okiya*, and move into that *okiya*'s dormitory. They live there with other members of the same *okiya* and their routines are strictly controlled. They learn manners and attend dance or music school. The training program is quite tough and many of the girls fail to become geisha. Those girls who pass, become *hangyoku* (probationary geisha), also called *maiko* in the Kansai area. During this period of on-the-job training, a full geisha acts as a mentor. Once a *hangyoku* is around twenty years old, she becomes a full geisha. She can then wear the traditional black kimono covered with exquisite paintings and have her hair in the unique geisha style.

芸者は本来パーティーで客をもてなす人です。第二次世界大戦以前は貧しい家の娘たちが置屋に売られていましたが、現代では希望者がやって来ます。希望者は置屋と呼ばれる芸者業と契約を交わし、置屋の寮に引っ越します。そこで同じ置屋に所属する少女たちと一緒に暮らします。スケジュールは厳しく管理されています。礼儀作法を学び、舞や音楽の学校に通います。稽古の課程はかなり厳しく、多くの少女が脱落します。稽古を終了した少女たちは半玉、または関西地方では舞妓と呼ばれる見習い芸者となります。研修期間中は1人前の芸者が後見人を務めます。半玉は20才を迎える頃に芸者となります。芸者になれば優美な絵が描かれた黒い着物を着て、芸者独特の髪型にすることができます。

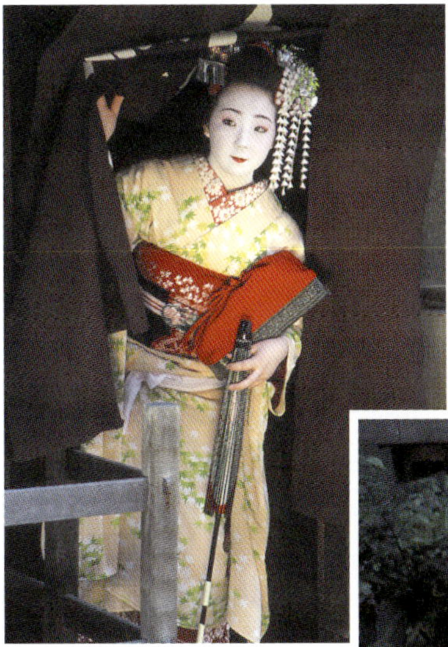

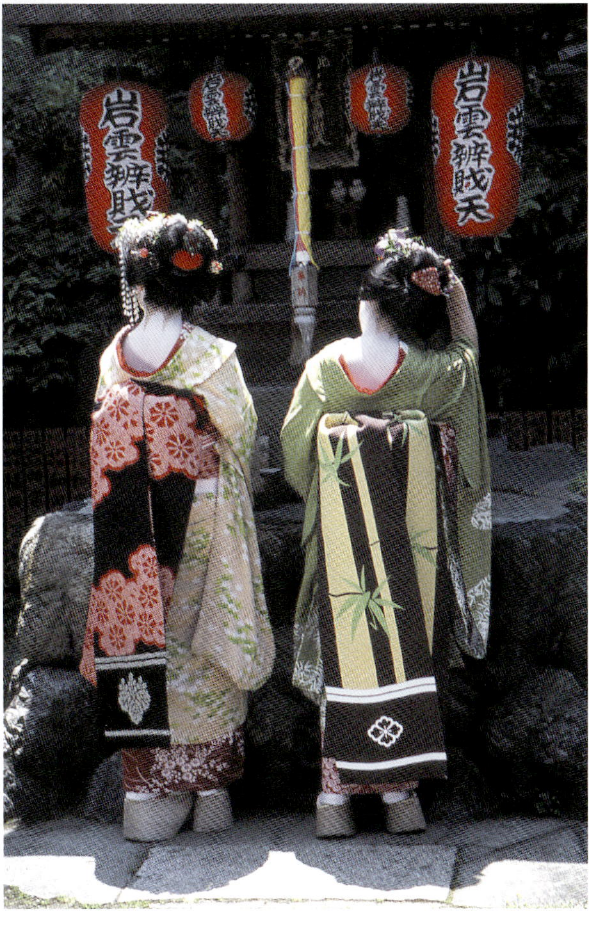
岩雲辨財天

HOUSING | 住宅

キーワード

somewhat 少し
in the suburbs of ～の郊外に
identical 全く同じ/そっくりの
multi-generational family 多世代家族
huge investment 多額の出資
rarely めったに～ない
move 引っ越す
apartment マンション
square meters 平方メートル

Modern Japanese houses look somewhat similar to Western houses, and in the suburbs of Japan one can find streets of similar or identical houses, just as in North America. A typical Japanese house has a kitchen, living room, dining room, Japanese-style room (tatami mat room) and two or three bedrooms. In multi-generational families, a young married couple sometimes lives with their children on the second floor, while their parents live on the first floor. In this case each floor has a kitchen and bathroom. Buying a house is a huge investment for Japanese people and once they have a house, they rarely sell it and move. Because the cost is so high, it is difficult to buy a house in the city these days. Therefore, most people who move to the city live in apartments. A family apartment is typically around a hundred square meters and has a living room, dining room, kitchen, and three bedrooms. For people living alone, the most common type of apartment has one room and a kitchen. These apartments are about twenty square meters.

現代の日本式住宅は欧米の住宅と少し似ているところもあり、郊外には北米の町並みと同じように、よく似た家やそっくりな家が建ち並んでいます。典型的な日本式住宅にはキッチン、リビング、ダイニング、和室、そして寝室が2つか3つあります。多世代家族の場合、若夫婦が子どもたちと2階に住み、その両親が1階に住むということもあります。この場合、それぞれの階にキッチンとバスルームがあります。住宅の購入は多額の出資なので、一旦手に入れると売却して引っ越すということはめったにありません。価格が非常に高いので、都市部で一戸建てを購入することは最近では難しくなっています。このため都市部に引っ越した人の多くはマンションに住んでいます。家族用マンションはだいたい100平米くらいの3LDKです。単身者用の一般的なマンションは1Kタイプです。これらは20平米くらいの広さです。

写真提供：積水化学工業株式会社

W4-MainPlan

イラスト提供：積水化学工業株式会社

81

INSIDE THE HOUSE　家の中

キーワード

entryway　玄関/入口
take off　脱ぐ
put on　履く/着る
equivalent　（相当する）もの
electric heater　電気ヒーター
attached to　～に取りつけられた
underside　底面
place　掛ける/置く
quilt　掛け布団
with one's legs stretched out　脚をのばして
underneath　～の下に
duvet　羽毛布団
be stuffed with　～が詰められている
wool　羊毛
feather　羽毛
air　空気にあてて乾かす
free ~ of . . .　～から…を除く
drain　排水溝
share　共有する
have a soak　（風呂に）つかる

Japanese houses usually have small entryways for taking off and putting on shoes, and most people wear slippers inside. Japanese kitchens, living rooms, and dining rooms, are not so different from their Western equivalents, but they are generally smaller.

Most houses in Japan don't have a central heating system. Instead, they have small heaters in most rooms. Many people have a *kotatsu*, which is a low table with a small electric heater attached to its underside. People place a blanket or quilt over the top and sit at the table with their legs stretched out underneath it.

たいていの日本の住宅には小さな玄関があり、そこで靴を脱いだり履いたりし、家の中ではスリッパを履く人が多いです。キッチン、リビング、ダイニングは欧米のものとさほど変わりませんが小さめです。

ほとんどの住宅にはセントラルヒーティングの設備がありません。代わりにだいたいどの部屋にも小さなヒーターがあります。多くの家庭にはこたつと呼ばれる、底面に小さな電気ヒーターがついた低いテーブルがあります。上から毛布や掛け布団を掛け、テーブルの下に脚をのばして座ります。

写真提供：積水化学工業株式会社

Although beds are becoming more popular, many people still use futon on beds. A futon has two parts, a mattress and a cover (like a duvet). Both of these are stuffed with wool, cotton or feathers. On sunny days people usually air their futon outside and beat them to free them of dust.

Japanese bathrooms have bathtubs of course, but there is also a washing space outside of the bathtub. It has a drain and is used for washing the body just before getting into the tub. It is important to be clean before entering the bath because families generally share the same bath water. Many Japanese people love having a relaxing soak in the tub.

ベッドを使う人も増えていますが、ベッドに布団を敷いて使っている人が多いです。布団は敷き布団と掛け布団(羽毛布団のようなもの)の2つがあります。両方とも羊毛、綿、羽毛などが詰められています。晴れた日には布団を外に干し、ほこりをはたきます。

日本の浴室には言うまでもなく浴槽がありますが、浴槽の外に体を洗うためのスペースもあります。ここには排水溝があり、浴槽に入る直前に体を洗うために使います。普通は家族が同じお湯を使うので、浴槽に入る前に体をきれいにしておかなければなりません。お湯につかってリラックスすることが大好きな日本人はたくさんいます。

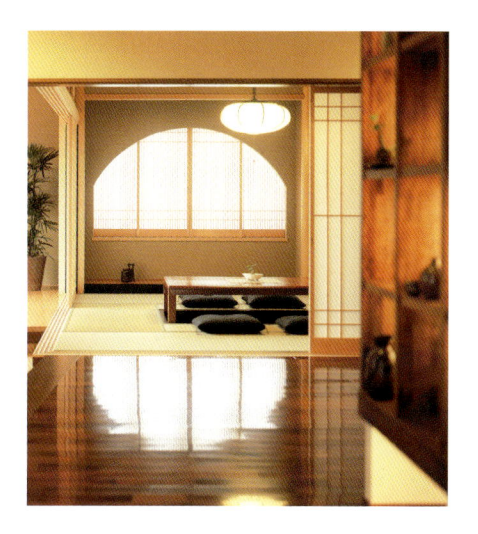

写真提供 左右とも：積水化学工業株式会社

HOT SPRINGS | 温泉

キーワード

bathe　入浴する
cure　治す
certain ailment　特定の病気
volcano　火山
healing property　効能
actual spring　源泉
boil　沸かす
mineral water　鉱水
outside bath　露天風呂
spectacular view　すばらしい景色
public bath　風呂屋/銭湯
Jacuzzi　泡風呂/ジャグジー
garden bath　露天風呂
sauna　サウナ

Most Japanese love bathing in hot springs, and many believe that the water can cure certain ailments. There are many volcanoes around Japan, and therefore many hot springs. Each hot spring is said to have its own healing property. Hot spring resorts or hotels either use water from an actual spring or they boil mineral water. Hot spring resorts have opened all over the country, and many hotels have outside baths offering spectacular views.

Public baths are also very common in Japan. They generally have Jacuzzis, garden baths, and saunas. At both hot springs and public baths, people actually wash their bodies before getting into the water. It is bad manners to use soap or towels in the bath itself.

大多数の日本人は温泉が大好きで、温泉水が特定の病気を治すと信じています。日本各地に火山があるので、温泉もたくさんあります。それぞれの温泉にそれぞれ違った効能があると言われています。温泉リゾートやホテルは源泉をそのまま、または鉱水を沸かして使っています。全国各地に温泉リゾートがあり、すばらしい景色を楽しめる露天風呂つきのホテルもたくさんあります。

風呂屋も日本ではよく知られています。風呂屋には泡風呂や露天風呂、サウナなどがあります。温泉でも風呂屋でも、お湯につかる前には体を洗います。浴槽の中で石けんやタオルを使うのはマナー違反です。

写真提供 上下とも：宮城県観光課

- Some baths are open to both men and women.
  混浴のところもあります。
- Some sick people stay at resorts for over a month to help them recover.
  持病を治すために温泉に1ヶ月以上滞在する人もいます。

MANGA | マンガ

キーワード

comic book コミックブック/マンガ本

be based on ～に基づく

incredibly 大変

episode 1回放映分

airing 放送

Manga, which are like comic books, and animation are important parts of modern Japanese culture. In fact, they have become famous around the world. Modern *manga* is based on the work of Tezuka Osamu who wrote many interesting stories and had many fans. Unlike in the West, the comic book style is very popular among adults.

The first animated TV series based on *manga* was *Tetsuwan Atom*, by Tezuka Osamu. (In North America it is known as *Astroboy*.) Animated TV shows are incredibly popular in Japan with over thirty, half-hour episodes airing each week. The majority of these series are based on *manga*. Animated movies are also very popular and many of them are based on popular TV series.

マンガ(コミックブックのようなもの)とアニメは現代日本文化の中の重要な一部分を担っています。事実、両方とも世界に知られています。現代の日本のマンガはおもしろいストーリーをたくさん書き、多くのファンがいた手塚治虫の作品が基礎になっています。欧米と違ってマンガは大人の間でも人気があります。

マンガに基づいた最初のテレビアニメは手塚治虫の「鉄腕アトム」でした。(北米では「アストロボーイ」として知られています)毎週1回30分ずつ放送されるテレビアニメは30本を超え、日本では大変人気があります。こういったシリーズのほとんどはマンガに基づいています。アニメ映画も大変人気があり、多くは人気テレビシリーズに基づいています。

写真提供:© 手塚プロダクション

CHARACTER PRODUCTS | キャラクター商品

キーワード	
along with	〜の他に
particular character	特定のキャラクター
related to	〜に関連した
strictly for	〜用だけに/〜のためだけに
character product market	キャラクター商品市場
key ring	キーホルダー
cell phone strap	携帯ストラップ
stuffed toy	ぬいぐるみ
stationary	文房具
as part of	〜の一環として
advertising strategy	広告戦略
ATM card	キャッシュカード

Just as in the West, collecting is a common hobby in Japan. Along with cards, mugs, and coins, character products are a popular item to collect. People, both children and adults, like a particular character and try to collect all things related to it. These characters usually come from TV shows, movies, *manga* and commercials, but many are also invented strictly for the character product market. Common products include key rings, cell phone straps, stuffed toys, stationary, cards and much more. Many serious companies now use characters as part of their advertising strategy. It is not uncommon to see characters on ATM cards or even painted on the sides of airplanes.

欧米のように何かを収集することは日本でも一般的な趣味です。カードやマグ、コインの収集の他にキャラクター商品も人気の高いコレクションアイテムです。子どもも大人も、特定のキャラクターが好きになって関連商品を全て集めようと努力します。

これらキャラクターはテレビ番組や映画、マンガ、コマーシャルから作られたものが多いのですが、キャラクター商品市場用だけに作られたものもたくさんあります。一般的な商品はキーホルダーや携帯ストラップ、ぬいぐるみ、文房具、カードなどです。今では堅いイメージの会社でも広告戦略の一環としてキャラクターを使っているところがたくさんあります。キャッシュカードや飛行機の機体にまでもキャラクターがついているのを目にすることは珍しくはありません。

写真提供:株式会社サンリオ ハローキティ30周年記念商品

CELL PHONES | 携帯電話

キーワード

communication tool
通信手段

organize　スケジュールを立てる

record　記録する

express one's personality
個性を表現する

extend to　～にまで及ぶ

various forms of
いろいろな形の

customization
カスタマイズ（各自に応じた仕様にすること）

decorate ~ with . . .
～を...で飾る

sticker　シール

display background
待ち受け画面

ring tone　着信音

carrying strap　ストラップ

integral part
欠くことのできない部分

imagine　考える

Cell phones are a central part of life in Japan. They are much more than simply a communication tool. People use them to express their personalities, as well as organize and record their lives. This starts with the selection of a phone and extends to various forms of customization, such as decorating it with stickers, using a personal photo as a display background, choosing the ring tone and adding a carrying strap.

Cell phones have become such an integral part of people's lives that it's hard for most to imagine life without them.

携帯電話は日本では生活の中心的役割をしています。単なる通信手段以上の存在になっています。スケジュールを立てたり記録したりすることはもちろん、個性を表現したりするのにも使います。これは機種を選ぶことから始まり、シールで飾ったり、待ち受け画面にプライベートな写真を設定したり、着信音を選んだり、ストラップをつけたりといったいろいろな「カスタマイズ」方法にまで及びます。携帯電話はこのように日本人の生活には欠かせない一部になっているので、もうそれなしの生活は考えられません。

PACHINKO | パチンコ

キーワード

huge 巨大な
brightly lit 派手にライトアップされた
pachinko parlor パチンコ店
cross between ~ and ... ~と...の中間
shoot 打つ
in diameter 直径で
travel through ~を通り抜ける
sort of ~のようなもの
maze 迷路
fall through ~に落ちる
uselessly 無駄に
spin around ぐるぐる回る
come up 出る
win the jackpot 大当たりになる
exchange ~ for ... ~を...と交換する
prize 景品

Huge, brightly lit *pachinko* parlors can be found all over Japan, in small towns as well as cities. *Pachinko* is like a cross between pinball and a slot machine. You play by shooting several small metal balls (about one centimeter in diameter) into the machine. The balls travel through a sort of maze in the machine. Most fall uselessly through the bottom, but a few fall through special holes in the middle. When that happens, the slot machine part of the game begins. Three pictures on the machine start spinning around and eventually stop. If all three pictures come up the same, the player wins the jackpot.

When you are finished playing, you can exchange your balls for prizes.

日本全国大きな町でも小さな町でも、巨大で派手にライトアップされたパチンコ店が見られます。パチンコはピンボールとスロットマシンの中間のようなものです。機械に直径1センチくらいの小さな金属の玉をいくつか入れ、それを打って遊びます。玉は機械に仕掛けられた迷路のようなものの中を通り抜けます。ほとんどの玉は無駄にそのまま底に落ちてしまいますが、いくつかは真ん中の特別な穴に落ちます。こうなるとスロットマシンのような状態に入ります。機械についている3つの絵がぐるぐる回り始め、徐々に止まります。もし3つの絵が揃えば大当たりです。遊び終わったら玉を景品と交換できます。

KARAOKE | カラオケ

キーワード

literally　文字通りに
empty orchestra
空っぽのオーケストラ
background music
伴奏/BGM
evolve　進化する
over the years
年月を重ねるにつれて
improve　良くする
be projected　映し出される
popularity　人気
lead to　〜をもたらす
boxlike room
ボックス状の部屋
soundproof　防音の
huge library
膨大なコレクション
function　機能
modify　加減する
pitch　音の高さ
echo　エコー

At first karaoke (meaning literally, "empty orchestra") was simply a tape with background music that allowed singers to practice. However, karaoke machines evolved over the years to use laser discs and CDs. This improved the sound quality and allowed video images to be projected while people sang. These days karaoke machines can even download songs from the internet. While karaoke was originally a form of entertainment in bars, its popularity led to a new type of business, the karaoke box. A karaoke box is a building with several small rooms. Each boxlike room is soundproof and has comfortable seats and a table. Groups of people can share one of these rooms for a more private karaoke experience. Karaoke boxes are also very cheap, and are therefore very popular with young people. Modern karaoke machines have huge libraries of songs and many special functions that allow users to modify speed, pitch and echo. Some machines can even score the singer's performance.

カラオケ(文字通り「空っぽのオーケストラ」という意味)は元々は歌手が練習するために使う伴奏だけが入ったテープのことでした。しかしカラオケは年月を重ねるにつれて進化し、レーザーディスクやCDも使われるようになりました。このため音質が良くなり、歌っている間にビデオ映像も映し出せるようになりました。今ではインターネットから曲をダウンロードできるカラオケ機器もあります。カラオケは元々はバーで楽しまれていたのですが、人気が高まったことでカラオケボックスという新しいビジネスが生まれました。カラオケボックスはいくつもの小さな部屋がある建物です。ボックス状の部屋はどれも防音されていて、座り心地の良いいすとテーブルがあります。グループでこの部屋を使うことで仲間だけでカラオケ体験をすることができます。またカラオケボックスは値段がとても安いので若者に大変人気があります。最新のカラオケ機器には膨大な歌のコレクションがあって、スピード、音の高さ、エコーを加減できる特別な機能もついています。機械によっては歌った人の得点まで出すことができます。

写真提供：ビッグエコー　八重洲本店

写真提供：ビッグエコー　北山店

SCHOOL LIFE | 学校生活

キーワード

compulsory education
義務教育

at six years of age　6才で

elementary school　小学校

spend　過ごす

junior college　短期大学

leather backpack
革のリュックサック

Dutch　オランダ語の

special occasion
特別な出来事

dress code　服装規定

be strictly regulated
厳しく規定されている

PE　体育

tuition　授業料

expense　経費

field trip　校外見学/遠足

supplementary material
副教材

As in North America, compulsory education in Japan begins at six years of age. Elementary school lasts six years after which children spend three years in junior high school. Most then go to high school for three years. After this, at the age of eighteen, many take either a two-year course in junior college, or a four-year university course.

北米と同じように、日本でも義務教育は6才から始まります。小学校6年間の後、中学校で3年間を過ごします。大多数はその後3年制の高校に進みます。卒業後18才で2年制の短期大学か4年制の大学に進む人も大勢います。

At most levels of education there is a school uniform. Elementary school students typically wear yellow hats and a leather backpack called a *randoseru* (from the Dutch word, ransel). The *randoseru* is a symbol of starting school and buying one is a special occasion. They are usually black for boys and red for girls, but other colors have recently become popular as well. Most junior high schools and high schools have their own uniform. Some schools are very serious about their dress codes, and things like skirt length, sock color, and bag style are strictly regulated. Schools also have a special uniform for PE classes.

Although all students must pay for their uniforms, the tuition and textbooks for compulsory education are free. There are, however, expenses for things like school lunches (about ￥200 a day), field trips and supplementary materials.

ほとんどの段階の学校で制服があります。小学生は黄色い帽子をかぶり、ランドセル(オランダ語のランセルに由来する)と呼ばれる革のリュックサックを背負っています。ランドセルは学校生活の始まりの象徴で、それを買うことは特別な出来事です。たいてい男の子用は黒、女の子用は赤ですが、近頃では他の色も人気があります。ほとんどの中学校、高校はそれぞれ独自の制服があります。服装規定にうるさい学校もあり、スカートの長さやソックスの色、かばんの形などが厳しく規定されています。体育用には専用のユニフォームがあります。

制服代は払わなければいけませんが、義務教育の間の授業料と教科書代は無償です。しかし給食費(1日200円程度)や遠足代、副教材費のような経費は必要です。

キーワード	
term	学期
short break	短い休み
calligraphy project	書道(の課題)
book report	読書感想文
diary	日記
assignment	課題
ceremony	式
principal	校長先生
diploma	卒業証書
school yearbook	卒業アルバム
hand out	手渡す
amusement park	遊園地
overseas trip	海外旅行
mid-term	中間(の)
final	期末(の)
entrance exam	入学試験
graduate from	卒業する
lead to	(ある結果に)つながる
regardless of	〜に関わらず
performance	成績
private educational institution	私立の教育機関

The beginning of the Japanese school year is in April and the end is in March. There are three terms in the year with short breaks between each term, in summer, winter and spring. However, most students have to do some kind of homework during the summer and winter breaks. Calligraphy projects, for example, are popular during winter vacation. Book reports and diaries are also popular assignments.

At the beginning and end of each term there is a ceremony at which the principal makes a speech. At the first ceremony of the new school year, in April, new students are welcomed. And at the end of the year there is a graduation ceremony at which diplomas and school yearbooks are handed out.

日本の学校は4月に始まり3月に終わります。1年は3学期に分かれ、それぞれの学期の間に夏、冬、春の短い休みがあります。ほとんどの生徒には夏休みと冬休みには何らかの宿題が出されます。例えば冬休みの代表的な宿題は書道です。読書感想文や日記もよくある課題です。

それぞれの学期の始まりと終わりに式があり、校長先生が話をします。4月に行われる新学年最初の式では新入生を歓迎します。学年度末には卒業式があり、卒業証書とアルバムが手渡されます。

Many schools have at least one fun field trip each year when, for example, they might go to an amusement park. Students go on at least one long trip in elementary, junior high and high school. This trip is normally to a famous place in Japan, like Kyoto, but some schools have overseas trips.

In junior high school and high school there are mid-term and final exams each term. The biggest worry for Japanese students and their parents are entrance exams. Universities and high schools all have entrance exams, as well as some junior high schools, elementary schools and even kindergartens. Graduating from good schools can lead to a good job, regardless of a student's performance. To help prepare for these exams, many children attend extra classes after school at private educational institutions called *juku* (cram schools).

どの学校にも毎年たいてい1回は楽しい遠足があり、遊園地などに出かけます。小・中・高校では1度は修学旅行に出かけます。普通は京都など日本の有名なところに行きますが、海外に出かける学校もあります。

中学校と高校ではそれぞれの学期に中間テストと期末テストがあります。生徒とその両親にとって最大の心配事は入学試験です。大学に入るにも高校に入るにも入学試験があります。中学校、小学校、幼稚園でさえ同様に試験があるところもあります。良い学校を卒業すると、生徒の成績に関わらず良い職につくことができるからです。多くの子どもたちは入学試験に備えて放課後、塾と呼ばれる私立の教育機関に通っています。

SUSHI 寿司

キーワード

broadly 大ざっぱに/広く
be classified into ～に分類される
refer to ～を指す
gut 内臓を取る
ferment 発酵させる
a portion of ほんの少しの
raw fish 生魚
on top 上に
fairly かなり
cucumber きゅうり
omelet 卵焼き
rolled in ～で巻いた
contain 入っている
combination 組み合わせ
seasoned 味つけした
pouch 袋
deep fried tofu 油揚げ
conveyor belt ベルトコンベヤー
cheap 安い
pay 支払う

There are many types of sushi, but they can all be broadly classified into two types, *nare-zushi* and *haya-zushi*. Although the word "sushi" can refer to either type, these days it usually refers to only *haya-zushi*.

Nare-zushi is very old and is made by gutting a fish and allowing it to ferment in cooked rice. Perhaps the most famous *nare-zushi* is *funa-zushi* from Shiga. *Funa-zushi* is still eaten, but these days sushi (*haya-zushi*) is much more popular.

Sushi, introduced in the Edo period (1603-1867), has a base of rice mixed with vinegar and the fish is not fermented. The first sushi was *nigiri*, a small portion of rice with a slice of raw fish on top. In the past it was fairly large, but these days is much smaller. Later, other types were introduced: *maki-zushi*, *chirashi-zushi*, *inari-zushi* and more. *Maki-zushi* is cucumber, *shiitake* mushroom, carrot and omelet rolled in rice and *nori* (see page 118). *Chirashi-zushi* contains a combination of cooked vegetables or seafood. And *inari-zushi* is vinegared rice in seasoned pouches of deep fried tofu.

寿司にはいろいろな種類がありますが、大ざっぱにはなれずしと早ずしの2つに分類できます。寿司と言えばこのどちらかですが、今日では普通は早ずしのことを指します。

なれずしの歴史は古く、内蔵を取り除いた魚をご飯に漬け、発酵させて作ります。1番有名ななれずしは滋賀県のふな寿司です。ふな寿司は現在も食べられていますが、最近では寿司(早ずし)の方がずっと知られています。

寿司は江戸時代(1603年〜1867年)に考案され、酢を混ぜたご飯をベースに発酵させない魚を使います。最初の寿司はにぎりで、ほんの少しのご飯の上に薄切りにした生魚をのせたものでした。昔のにぎり寿司はかなり大きなものでしたが、現在のものはずっと小さくなっています。後に巻き寿司、ちらし寿司、いなり寿司なども作られるようになりました。巻き寿司はきゅうり、しいたけ、にんじん、卵焼きなどをご飯とのりで巻いたものです。ちらし寿司は調理した野菜や魚介類が入ったもので、いなり寿司は味つけした油揚げの袋に寿司飯を詰めたものです。

Chirashi-zushi

Maki-zushi and *inari-zushi*

Nigiri-zushi

- Conveyor belt sushi restaurants, called *kaiten-zushi*, are really popular and cheap places for dinner. Customers choose the sushi they want, paying a set price for each plate when they are finished.
  回転寿司と呼ばれる、ベルトコンベヤーにのった寿司が出てくるレストランは大変人気があり、安く夕食がとれるところです。客は食べたい寿司を選んで、食後に皿毎に決められている値段を支払います。
- Sushi chefs are usually men.
  寿司職人は男性が多いです。

SASHIMI | 刺身

キーワード

confused with	〜と勘違いした
white fish flesh	白身魚
thinly	薄く
thicker	厚めの
shredded	細かく刻んだ
seaweed	わかめ/海藻
herb	ハーブ
be served with	〜と一緒に出される
mask	隠す
fishy smell	生臭いにおい
assist digestion	消化を助ける
make for	〜に役立つ
presentation	見栄え
season	薬味をのせる
dip	つける
lightly	少し
soy sauce	醤油

Sashimi, often confused with sushi, is raw seafood. The eating of *sashimi* began some eight hundred years ago in Japan and has been evolving ever since. White fish flesh is usually sliced thinly, while red fish flesh is cut into thicker pieces. Typically, shredded *daikon* (white radish), cucumber or seaweed, and the herb *oba* is served with *sashimi*. *Wasabi* (Japanese horseradish) or ginger is also served. All of these help to mask the fishy smell, improve the taste, and assist digestion. They also make for a nicer presentation. The best way to eat *sashimi* is to season it and dip it lightly in soy sauce.

刺身はよく寿司と勘違いされますが、生の魚介類のことです。日本で刺身が食べられるようになったのは800年ほど前からで、以後いろいろと変化してきました。たいてい白身魚は薄く切り、赤身魚は厚めに切ります。一般的には細かく刻んだ大根、きゅうり、わかめ、大葉などが刺身と一緒に出されます。わさびやしょうがもつけ合わせます。これらは生臭いにおいを消し、風味を良くして消化を助ける役割があります。また、見栄えを良くするのにも役立ちます。刺身をおいしく食べるコツは薬味をのせ、醤油に少しつけることです。

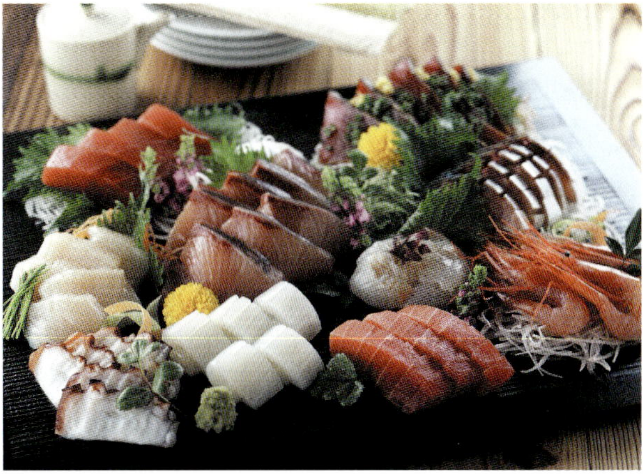

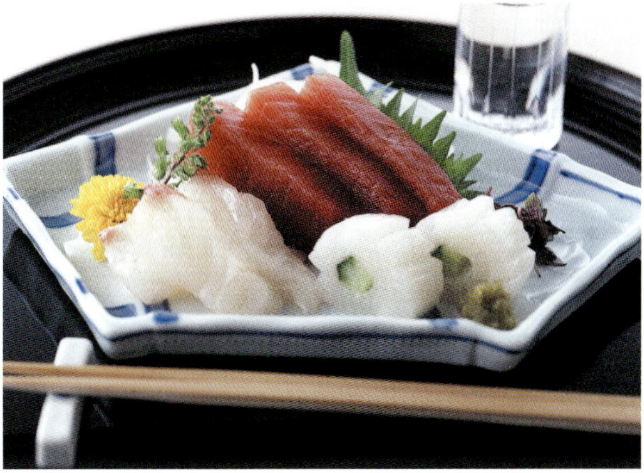

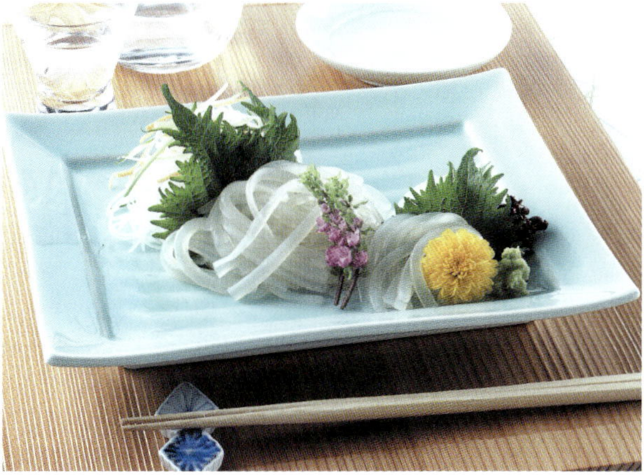

TEMPURA 天ぷら

キーワード

be around for a long time	かなり昔からある
deep fry	揚げる
in batter	ころもをつけて
watery	水気の多い
heat	熱する
salad oil	サラダ油
~ degrees centigrade	(摂氏)~度
ingredient	材料
for a short period of time	短時間
serving	~人分
prawn	エビ
shell	殻をむく
tail	尾
attached	ついたまま
belly	腹
prevent	~させない
scallop	ほたて貝
pat dry	水気を切る
horse mackerel	アジ
back	背
lengthwise	縦に
remove	取り除く
center bone	背骨

Tempura has been around for a long time, but only became popular about 150 years ago. It is made from seafood or vegetables deep fried in batter. Smaller, white-fleshed fish are usually used for tempura. Vegetables can also be used, but usually not watery ones like cucumber. It is simple to make. Simply heat salad oil to 170 degrees centigrade and fry the ingredients for a short period of time. Tempura is usually eaten with a soy-based sauce.

天ぷらはかなり昔から存在しましたが、一般的に広まったのは150年ほど前からです。魚介類や野菜にころもをつけて揚げたものです。天ぷらには小さな白身魚がよく使われます。また野菜類も使いますが、きゅうりのように水気の多いものは使いません。作り方は簡単です。サラダ油を170度くらいに熱して、材料を短時間で揚げます。天ぷらは普通、醤油味のつゆにつけて食べます。

Ingredients (four servings)

Seafood: 8 prawns (shell and clean with tails still attached and with three or four small cuts across the belly to prevent curling), 4 scallops (wash and pat dry), 4 small horse mackerels (cut the back lengthwise, remove center bone, head and entrails, pat dry)

Vegetables: 2 eggplants (wash and cut into quarters, soak in water to remove bitterness, then dry), 8 *shiitake* mushrooms (clean, remove stems and score a cross on top), 1 sweet potato (peel and cut into thick slices), 1 medium onion (peel and cut in half, cut across into slices and pierce with toothpicks or bamboo skewers to hold together)

材料（4人分）

魚介類： エビ8尾（尾をつけたまま殻と背わたを取り、曲がらないよう腹に3つ4つ小さく切れ目を入れる）、ほたて貝4個（洗って水気を切っておく）、小アジ4匹（背を縦に切って広げ、背骨、頭、はらわたを取り除いて洗い、水気を切る）

野菜： なす2本（洗ってから四つ切りにし、水に漬けてあくを取り水気を切る）、しいたけ8枚（洗って石づきを取り、上に十字の切れ目を入れる）、さつまいも1本（皮をむいて厚めにスライスする）、たまねぎ中1個（皮をむいて半分に切り、横向きに厚めにスライスする、バラバラにならないよう楊枝や竹串を刺しておく）

entrails	はらわた
eggplant	なす
cut into quarters	四つ切りする
soak	漬ける
stem	石づき/茎/へた
bitterness	あく/苦み
score a cross	十字に切り込みを入れる
peel	（皮を）むく
pierce	刺す
toothpick	楊枝
bamboo skewer	竹串
bring to a boil	沸騰させる
strain	こす
set aside	置いておく
flour	小麦粉
whisk	混ぜる/泡立てる
item	具
gently	そっと
slip	入れる
golden	きつね色になる
drain	（水気や油を）切る
attractively	美しく
condiment	薬味
grated	すりおろした
ginger	しょうが

Ten-tsuyu (soy-based sauce): 1/4 cup *mirin* (sweet sake), 1/4 cup soy sauce, 1/3 cup *katsuobushi* (see page 118), 1 cup water

(1. Heat the *mirin*. 2. Add the other ingredients and bring to a boil. 3. Strain and set aside.)

Batter: 1 egg, 3/4 cup of cold water, 1 cup of flour, salad oil (for deep-frying)

(1. Whisk the egg and cold water in a bowl. 2. Add the flour and mix lightly.)

天つゆ：みりん1/4カップ、醤油1/4カップ、かつお節1/3カップ、水1カップ
（1. みりんを温める。 2. 他の材料も入れて沸騰させる。 3. こして置いておく。）
ころも：卵1個、冷水3/4カップ、小麦粉1カップ、サラダ油（揚げる時）
（1. ボウルで卵と冷水を混ぜる。 2. さらに小麦粉を入れ軽く混ぜる。）

Directions

1. Heat oil to 170 degrees centigrade.
2. Fry the vegetables first. Dip each item in the batter then gently slip it into oil. Turn a few times until golden. Remove from oil and place on a rack to drain.
3. Repeat with the seafood.
4. Arrange attractively on a plate and serve with condiments (grated *daikon* or grated fresh ginger) and *ten-tsuyu*.

作り方

1. 油を170度に熱する。
2. まず野菜を揚げる。具をころもにつけ、油にそっと入れる。きつね色になるまで具を何回か返す。油から上げ、油をよく切る。
3. 魚介類も同じようにする。
4. 皿に美しく盛りつけ、薬味（大根おろしやおろししょうが）、天つゆと一緒に出す。

NABEMONO | 鍋物

キーワード

quite uniquely	かなり独特に
boiling	沸騰している
pot	鍋
participate in	～に参加する
communal	共用の
sesame sauce	ごまだれ
soy and vinegar sauce	ポン酢
block	かたまり
bite-size	一口サイズの
packet	パック
devil's tongue yam	こんにゃく芋
leek	長ねぎ/ねぎ
diagonally	斜めに
ounce	オンス(重量の単位、1オンス約28グラム)
edible	食用の
chrysanthemum	菊
suet	ラード
5 tablespoons ~	大さじ5杯の～
melt	溶かす
brown	焦げ目をつける
pour	注ぐ
break	割る
beat	ほぐす/かき混ぜる

Nabemono is very much like stew, but the way it is served and prepared is quite uniquely Japanese. It is usually eaten in a group. A boiling pot of soup or water is brought to the table with plates of ingredients. The members of the group all participate in the cooking of the ingredients and then eat from that one communal pot.

There are two main varieties of *nabemono*, those cooked in soup, and those cooked in boiling water. The most popular type of soup *nabemono* is *sukiyaki* (beef and vegetables), but there are others, such as *yosenabe* (which also includes seafood). *Shabushabu* is probably the most common type of boiling water *nabemono*. Thinly sliced beef is dipped into boiling water and then dipped into sesame sauce or soy and vinegar sauce. Other types of boiling water *nabemono* are *yudofu* (see page 108), and *chirinabe* (seafood and vegetables).

鍋物はシチューによく似ていますが、もてなし方や作り方はかなり日本独特のものです。普通は何人かで食べます。沸騰しただしまたは湯が入った鍋と材料をのせた皿を一緒にテーブルに出します。全員が調理に加わり、その1つの鍋から分け合っていただきます。

鍋物には予め味のついているものと水炊きするものの2種類があります。予め味がついている鍋物の代表的なものはすき焼き(牛肉や野菜)ですが、他に寄せ鍋(魚介類を加えたもの)があります。しゃぶしゃぶは水炊きする鍋物の代表です。薄くスライスした牛肉をお湯にくぐらせ、ごまだれやポン酢につけていただきます。水炊きする鍋物には他に湯豆腐やちり鍋(魚介類と野菜)があります。

Yudofu

SUKIYAKI/すき焼き

Ingredients (four servings)
1 pound sliced beef sirloin, tenderloin or rump, 1 block tofu cut into bite-size pieces (grilled tofu is best), 8 to 12 *shiitake* mushrooms (remove stems), 1 packet *konnyaku* noodles (a kind of noodle made from devil's tongue yam), 2 leeks (cut diagonally into pieces about five centimeters long), 10 ounces edible chrysanthemum leaves, suet, 4 eggs

sauce: 1/3 cup soy sauce, 1/3 cup *mirin*, 1/3 cup *katsuobushi* (see page 118), 1 cup water, 5 tablespoons sugar

材料（4人分）
サーロイン、テンダーロイン、ランプいずれかのスライス1ポンド、豆腐1丁を一口サイズに切る（焼き豆腐ならなお良い）、しいたけ8〜12枚（石づきを取り除く）、糸こんにゃく（こんにゃく芋から作った麺）1パック、長ねぎ2本（斜めに5センチくらいの長さに切る）、春菊10オンス、ラード、卵4個
わりした：醤油1/3カップ、みりん1/3カップ、かつお節1/3カップ、水1カップ、砂糖大さじ5杯

Directions
1. Prepare the ingredients and arrange attractively on a large plate.
2. Prepare the sauce. Mix the ingredients and bring to a boil in a saucepan. Strain and set aside.
3. Heat a pan and melt the suet.
4. Add beef slices and brown on both sides.
5. Add small amounts of other ingredients and pour sauce over them about 0.5 centimeters deep.
6. Break a raw egg into a bowl and beat it. Then take cooked ingredients from the sukiyaki pan, dip them in the egg and eat.

作り方
1. 材料を切って大皿に見映えよく並べる。
2. わりしたを作る。材料を鍋に入れて混ぜ、沸騰させて置いておく。
3. 鍋を熱してラードを溶かす。
4. 牛肉のスライスを鍋に入れ、両面焦げ目がつくまで火を通す。
5. 残りの材料を少しずつ鍋に入れ、作っておいたわりしたを0.5センチほどの深さまで注ぐ。
6. 各自の取り鉢に卵を割りほぐし、具をそれにつけて食べる。

OKONOMIYAKI | お好み焼き

キーワード

iron hot plate	鉄板
combination of ~ and ...	~と...の組み合わせ
pour	流す
preheated	予め熱した
thick sauce	とろみのあるソース
powdered seaweed	青のり
sprinkle	ふりかける
regional variety	地域による違い
pile	積み重ねる
directly off	~から直接
boiled	ゆでた
octopus	タコ

In Japan there are a variety of foods cooked on iron hot plates. One of these is *okonomiyaki*. It's like a combination of pancakes and pizza. The base is a batter made of flour, water and eggs with shredded cabbage. The batter is then poured on to a preheated hot plate and cooked very much like a pancake. Thin slices of pork are then added, a thick sauce is poured on, and finally *katsuobushi* (see page 118) and powdered seaweed are sprinkled over the top.

There are several regional varieties of *okonomiyaki*. In the Kansai area for example, the vegetables are mixed with the batter and then cooked, but in Hiroshima, the batter is cooked separately and then the vegetables are piled on top. In the Kanto area there is a similar food called *monjayaki*, which is softer and usually eaten directly off the hot plate. Another hot plate food, *takoyaki*, is popular in the Kansai area. *Takoyaki* uses the same basic batter, but also contains boiled octopus. It is cooked into a ball shape using a special hot plate.

日本には鉄板の上で焼く料理がいろいろあります。その1つはお好み焼きです。パンケーキとピザを足して割ったようなものです。小麦粉、水、卵を合わせた生地に、刻んだキャベツを加えたものがベースになります。予め熱しておいた鉄板に生地を流し、パンケーキを作る時のように焼きます。スライスした豚肉をのせ、とろみのあるソースをかけ、最後にかつお節と青のりをふりかけます。

お好み焼きは地方によって違いがあります。例えば関西では生地と野菜を混ぜてから焼きますが、広島では生地を先に流し、その上に野菜を積み重ねます。関東ではもんじゃ焼きというお好み焼きに似た食べ物があり、お好み焼きより柔らかく、鉄板から直接食べます。他に鉄板を利用した料理にたこ焼きがありますが、これは関西でよく食べられています。お好み焼きと同じ生地を使いますが、ゆでたタコが入っています。専用の鉄板でボール型に焼きます。

Kansai style *okonomiyaki*

YATAI 屋台

キーワード
- originate　始まる
- eating out　外食
- charcoal grilled　炭火焼きにした
- skewer　串
- simmered in　～で煮込んだ
- kelp based stock　昆布だし
- cart　荷車
- customer　客
- at a time　1度に

Yatai (food stalls) are usually open at night. They originated in the Edo period (1603-1867), when eating out was very popular. Initially, sushi and tempura were the foods of choice at yatai, but these days, *yakitori* (charcoal grilled chicken on a skewer), *oden* (beef, vegetables, and egg simmered in a kelp based stock and served with mustard seasoning), and *ramen* (see page 110) are also popular *yatai* dishes. *Yatai* are typically carts, but trucks and vans are also used. There is usually a counter around the kitchen area, which is used as a table by the customers. Generally, about four customers can sit around one *yatai* at a time.

屋台はたいてい夜に営業しています。外食が流行した江戸時代(1603年〜1867年)に始まりました。最初は寿司や天ぷらの屋台が出されていましたが、最近では焼き鳥(串に刺した鶏肉の炭火焼き)やおでん(牛肉、野菜、卵を昆布だしで煮込み、からしをつけて食べる)、ラーメンが屋台のメニューとして人気があります。典型的な屋台は荷車ですが、トラックやバンの屋台もあります。調理台の周りにカウンターがあり、客がテーブルとして使います。1つの屋台に1度に4人くらいが座ることができます。

Yakitori

Oden

IZAKAYA 居酒屋

キーワード

alcoholic beverage
アルコール飲料

light food　軽い食事

designed for
～用(に考えられた)

reserved　遠慮がちの

loud　騒々しい

rival　ひけをとらない

British　イギリスの

Izakaya are bar-restaurants usually open only in the evenings and at night. They serve alcoholic beverages and light food or snacks. People typically go as a group, so *izakaya* usually have tatami rooms with low tables designed for groups of guests. Although Japanese people are generally quite reserved at work or at home, an *izakaya* is one place they can relax. They may be the loudest places in Japan and the noise level certainly rivals any British pub or American bar.

居酒屋は夕方か夜だけ営業しているレストランバーです。アルコール類や軽い食事、スナックなどを出します。たいていはグループで行くので、グループ用の座卓を置いた和室がいくつかあります。一般的に日本人は職場や家庭ではとても控え目ですが、居酒屋はリラックスできる場の1つです。居酒屋は日本で1番と言っていいくらい騒々しい場所で、この騒がしさはイギリスのパブやアメリカのバーにひけをとらないほどです。

SOYBEAN PRODUCTS | 大豆製品

キーワード

soybean　大豆

nutritious food
栄養のある食品

make great use of
よく利用する

mash　つぶす

paste　ペースト

pulp　果肉（おから）

liquid　液体（豆乳）

sticky　ねばねばした

smelly　においがある

get a lot of attention
大きな注目を浴びる

wheat　小麦

foundation　基盤

cuisine　料理

steamed　蒸した

fermenting agent　発酵剤

grain　穀物

date back to　〜にさかのぼる

be categorized by
〜で分類される

The soybean is one of the most nutritious foods in the world, and the Japanese make great use of it. Soybeans are the main ingredient of tofu, *natto*, *shoyu* and *miso*.

Tofu is made from soybeans that have been soaked in water, mashed into a paste, boiled and then separated into pulp and liquid. Various thickeners are then added to the liquid to create different types of tofu. *Momen-dofu* is drier and harder. *Kinugoshi-dofu* is softer and eaten uncooked or added to *nabemono* (see page 102) or *miso* soup (see page 114).

Natto is fermented soybeans. It's sticky and smelly, so while some people love it, others hate it. For a long time it was not popular in the Kansai area, but it has gotten a lot of attention recently as a health food and is growing in popularity. It is usually seasoned with *shoyu*, mustard, *katsuobushi* (see page 118) or leeks.

大豆は世界的に最も栄養のある食品の1つで、日本人はよく利用します。大豆は豆腐、納豆、醤油、味噌の主原料です。

豆腐は水に浸した大豆をつぶしてペースト状にし、加熱してからおからと豆乳に分けます。いろいろな凝固剤を豆乳に加えると、種類の違った豆腐ができます。木綿豆腐は水気が少なく堅いです。絹ごし豆腐は柔らかく、そのまま食べたり、鍋物や味噌汁に入れたりします。

納豆は大豆を発酵させたものです。ねばねばしてにおいがあるので、非常に好んで食べる人もいますが苦手な人もいます。以前は関西ではあまり食べられていませんでしたが、健康食品として大きく注目を浴び、最近ではよく食べられるようになりました。醤油、からし、かつお節、ねぎなどの薬味を混ぜて食べます。

Shoyu

Miso

Shoyu is made by fermenting a mixture of soybeans and wheat in salty water for over a year. *Shoyu* has existed for over a thousand years and is the foundation of Japanese cuisine. There are several types. *Usukuchi-shoyu* is very thin. It's popular in the Kansai area and is good for cooking vegetables. *Koikuchi-shoyu* is a popular thick soy sauce. *Tamari* is another type of very thick soy sauce and is usually eaten with *sashimi*.

Miso is a paste made by mixing steamed soybeans with salt, *koji* (a fermenting agent), and sometimes a grain (rice, wheat, etc.). *Miso* dates back to the seventh century and many types have evolved. *Miso* is now categorized by color: red, white or mixed; by taste: sweet or salty; and by ingredients: rice, wheat or soybeans.

醤油は大豆と小麦を塩水に混ぜて仕込み、1年以上発酵させたものです。醤油の歴史は千年以上あり日本料理の基盤です。種類がいくつかあります。淡口醤油は色が薄く、関西地方でよく使われ、野菜の煮物に適しています。濃口醤油は色の濃い一般的な醤油です。たまりはとても濃い醤油で、刺身を食べる時に使います。

味噌は蒸した大豆と塩、麹（発酵剤）、時には穀物類（米、小麦など）を混ぜ合わせて造るペーストです。味噌の歴史は7世紀にさかのぼり、現在までいろいろな種類が造られてきました。現在では色：赤、白、合わせ、味：甘口、辛口、材料：米、小麦、大豆などによって分類されています。

Tofu

Natto

NOODLES 麺類

キーワード

broth
(肉、野菜などを煮だした)スープ

fry 炒める

feel well 体調が良い

buckwheat
そば(の実)/そば粉

New Year's Eve 大晦日

slightly 少し

alkali water
アルカリ水(かんすい)

pull 引きのばす

to this day 現在でも

Styrofoam 発泡スチロール

freeze-dried state
フリーズドライ状態

Noodles are very popular in Japan, and there are three major types: *udon*, *soba*, and *ramen*.

Udon is made from flour, salt and water and there are several varieties, like *kishimen* (flat noodles) and *somen* (thin noodles). *Udon* is eaten in several ways, but the most popular is to cook it in or dip it in a broth. It can also be fried (*yaki udon*), or cooked in *nabemono* (see page 102). People often eat cold *udon* in the summer. It is easily digested and therefore often eaten when people aren't feeling well.

Soba is made from buckwheat and water. *Soba* noodles, like *udon* noodles, are commonly served with or in a broth. They are often eaten on New Year's Eve for good luck. It is perhaps most popular in the Kanto area, where it is generally served with a slightly thicker broth than in the Kansai area.

麺類は日本ではとても人気があります。うどん、そば、ラーメンの3つが主な種類です。うどんは小麦粉、塩、水が原料で、きしめん(平らな麺)やそうめん(細い麺)などいろいろな種類があります。食べ方もいろいろですが、最も一般的なものはだしをかけたり、だしにつけたりする食べ方です。また炒めたり(焼きうどん)、鍋物に入れたりもします。夏には冷たいうどんをよく食べます。また消化が良いので体調が良くない時にもうどんをよく食べます。

そばはそば粉と水が原料です。そばはうどんと同じように、だしをかけたりつけたりして食べます。大晦日に幸運を祈って食べることもよくあります。そばはおそらく関東地方で最もよく食べられています。関西と比べてだしは少し濃いめです。

Udon

Soba

Ramen is similar to *udon*. It is also made from flour. However, it is made using alkali water and is also pulled into a thinner shape than *udon*. Although originally from China, *ramen* dishes have truly become Japanese. *Ramen*'s popularity increased even more when in the 1950s instant *ramen* was invented.

The first instant *ramen* product was *Chicken Ramen* and it is still sold to this day. There are two types of instant *ramen*. One is a cup (usually Styrofoam) containing all the ingredients (noodles, vegetables, etc.) in a freeze-dried state. Preparing this type is simple. Just pour boiling water into the cup and wait about three minutes. The other type of instant *ramen* has separate packaging for the noodles and powdered broth. These are mixed together in boiling water and other ingredients can be added.

ラーメンはうどんに似ています。小麦が原料ですが、かんすいを使用し、うどんより細く生地をのばします。中国から伝えられたものですが、ラーメンは日本の国民食になりました。1950年代にインスタントラーメンが作られて以来ますます人気が高まりました。最初のインスタントラーメンはチキンラーメンで、現在も販売されています。インスタントラーメンには2種類あります。1つはカップ（通常発泡スチロールでできている）にフリーズドライ状態の材料（麺、野菜など）が全て入っているものです。このタイプの作り方は簡単です。カップに沸騰したお湯を入れ、3分ほど待ちます。別の種類のインスタントラーメンは麺とスープが別に入っています。沸騰したお湯の中に入れ、一緒にかき混ぜます。他の食材などを加えることもできます。

Ramen

RICE 米

キーワード

rice cultivation 稲作
quickly spread すぐに広まる
relative 相対的な
region 領土
be gauged by ～によって評価される
average 平均の
annual 年間の
rice crop 米の収穫量
short grain (粒の)短い米
staple food 主食
a wide variety of いろいろな種類の
triangular in shape 三角形をしている
wrap 巻く
pound (もちを)つく
sweet bean paste 小豆あん
ceremonial occasions 特別な行事
cooked topping 調理された具
eel うなぎ
vacuum-packed 真空パックの

Rice cultivation probably began in Japan over two thousand years ago and quickly spread across all four main islands. In the past the relative power of each region was gauged by the size of its average annual rice crop.

All Japanese rice is of the short grain variety, but there are many brands, with a different taste.

Rice is the staple food of Japan and is used to make a wide variety of foods and products. One of the most common uses is to make *onigiri*. Usually referred to as rice balls in English, *onigiri* are in fact typically triangular in shape. Inside you might find *umeboshi* (see page 115), *konbu* (see page 118), salmon or tuna, and *nori* (see page 118) is wrapped around the outside.

Another rice food is *mochi*. It is made from steamed rice that has been pounded into a thick paste. It is typically added to soup or cooked with sweet bean paste, and is sometimes eaten on ceremonial occasions.

Donburi is a rice dish served in a large bowl (also called a *donburi*). It is basically rice with some sort of cooked topping. *Unadon*, for example, is rice with eel; *gyudon* is rice and beef; and *oyakodon* is rice with chicken and eggs.

日本で稲作が始められたのは2千年以上前で、主な4島にすぐに広まったと言われています。昔は各領土の権力の優劣は、米の収穫量の年間平均で評価されていました。

日本の米は全て短い米ですが、いろいろと味の違う銘柄がたくさんあります。

米は日本の主食で非常にたくさんの食べ物や製品に利用されています。1番よく使われるのはおにぎりの材料としてです。英語ではライスボールと言われていますが、おにぎりは普通は三角形をしています。梅干し、昆布、さけ、ツナなどを中に入れ、のりで巻きます。

他に米を使った食べ物としてはもちがあります。米を蒸し、ついて堅めのペーストにします。汁物に入れたり、小豆あんと料理したり、特別な行事などの際に食べたりします。

丼は大きな鉢(これも丼と言います)に入れて出されます。基本的にはご飯の上に調理された具がのっています。例えばうな丼はご飯とうなぎ、牛丼はご飯と牛肉、親子丼はご飯と鶏肉と卵の組み合わせです。

Onigiri

Mochi

Mochi

Unadon

Gyudon

Oyakodon

- Cooked rice is called *gohan* and uncooked rice, *kome*.
  炊いた米はご飯と呼び、炊いていないものを米と呼びます。
- *Gohan* is sold in vacuum-packed bags at convenience stores, supermarkets and department stores.
  真空パックの袋に入ったご飯は、コンビニ、スーパー、デパートなどでも売られています。

SOUP 汁物

キーワード

grilled fish　焼き魚
cooked dish　煮物
shellfish　貝
diet　食事

Traditionally, Japanese meals had three dishes: *sashimi*, grilled fish, a cooked dish, and soup. Japanese soups fall into two categories: *sumashi* (clear soup), and *miso*-based soup. *Sumashi* is made from a kelp or *katsuobushi* (see page 118) stock and usually contains salt and some type of white-fleshed fish or shellfish. *Miso* soup is made from *miso* mixed with soup stock and may contain seaweed, seafood, meat, tofu (see page 108) or vegetables. Today *miso* soup and rice are the staple foods of the Japanese diet.

伝統的な日本の食事は刺身、焼き魚、煮物と汁物の1汁3菜でした。日本の汁物は2種類に分けられます。すまし（澄んだスープ）と味噌汁です。すましは昆布やかつお節のだしから作られ、塩と白身魚や貝類が入っています。味噌汁はだしと味噌を合わせたもので、わかめ、魚介類、肉、豆腐や野菜が入っています。現在では味噌汁とご飯は日本人の食事に欠かせないものになっています。

Sumashi

Miso soup

PICKLES 漬物

キーワード

local ingredients 地元の食材
pickling juice 漬汁
rice bran 米ぬか
pickled in ～に漬けた
mid-summer 真夏
last a long time 長持ちする
health benefits 健康に良いこと
time consuming 時間がかかる
prepared pickling juice 漬物の素

Pickles are very popular in Japan and are made from a wide variety of fruits and vegetables. They are generally made from local ingredients, so each area has different pickles. The pickling juice may contain salt, vinegar, *miso*, rice bran or *shoyu* (see page 108). The most popular pickles are *takuan*, which is dried *daikon* (white radish) pickled in salt and rice bran, and *umeboshi*, which is *ume* (a kind of sour plum) pickled in salt, and dried in mid-summer. It lasts a long time and is said to have great health benefits. Making pickles is time consuming, so many people buy prepared pickling juice.

漬物は日本で広く食べられていて、いろいろな種類のくだものや野菜から作られています。一般的に地元の材料が使われるので、その地方独特の漬物があります。漬汁には塩、酢、味噌、米ぬかや醤油などがあります。代表的な漬物はたくあんで、これは干した大根を塩と米ぬかに漬けたものです。梅干しは梅の実を塩漬けして、真夏に乾燥させます。長持ちしますし、健康にも良いとされています。漬物を漬けるのには時間がかかるので漬物の素を買う人もいます。

Takuan

Umeboshi

BENTO 弁当

キーワード

equivalent　相当するもの
brown bag lunch
ブラウンバッグランチ（茶色の紙袋に入れたお弁当）
central figure　中心
come in
〜に入って（売られて）いる
disposable　使い捨ての
separate compartment
仕切られた部分
local speciality　地方の特産物
arrange　手を加える
skin　皮

Bento is the Japanese equivalent of the Western brown bag lunch. It is a central figure in Japanese food culture. It typically contains rice and small portions of several dishes such as fried chicken, vegetables, fish, and many more. Store-bought *bento* comes in disposable plastic trays with separate compartments for each dish, but many people have their own lunch box for homemade *bento*.

Bento can be bought at convenience stores (*konbini bento*), department stores (*depa-chika bento*) or train stations (*eki ben*). *Depa-chika bento* are usually more expensive and look nicer than *konbini bento*. *Eki ben* usually contains local specialities.

Another type of *bento*, *makunouchi bento*, comes from Edo period (1603-1867) theaters. It is still popular today and can now be bought in convenience stores, supermarkets and *bento* shops.

弁当は欧米のブラウンバッグランチに相当します。弁当は日本の食文化の中心です。ご飯、から揚げ、野菜、魚などのおかずが少量ずつ入っています。店頭販売の弁当は、それぞれのおかずが別々に入れられるように、仕切られたプラスティックの使い捨て容器に入っています。しかし家で作る弁当用の弁当箱を持っている人もたくさんいます。

弁当はコンビニ（コンビニ弁当）、デパート（デパ地下弁当）、駅（駅弁）でも買うことができます。デパ地下弁当はコンビニ弁当よりも値段が高く、見た目もきれいです。駅弁はその地方の特産物が使われています。

他に幕の内弁当があり、これは江戸時代（1603年〜1867年）に劇場で食べられていました。今もコンビニ、スーパー、弁当屋で買うことができます。

- *Bento* made by one's wife is sometimes called *aisai bento* (a loving wife's *bento*).
  奥さんが作った弁当のことを愛妻弁当と言うこともあります。
- *Bento* usually look very nice.
  弁当は見た目も非常にきれいに作られていることが多いです。
- Many parents arrange the food to look nice for their children. For example, they might peel an apple skin to look like a rabbit or cut a sausage to look like an octopus.
  たいていの親は、子ども用の弁当は材料に少し手を加えてかわいらしくしてあります。例えばうさぎに見えるようにりんごの皮をむいたり、タコに見えるようにウインナーに切り込みを入れたりします。

COMMON INGREDIENTS | 一般的な食材

キーワード

bonito　かつお

oily　脂ののった

purchase　買う

plain　味のついていない

root　根

hot　辛い

reputed　（～という）評判の

kill bacteria　殺菌する

smoke　薫製する/あぶる

chop up　切り刻む

spread out　広げる

There are several very common ingredients in Japanese cuisine. Among them are soup stock, *katsuobushi*, *nori* and *wasabi*.

Japanese soup stock is typically made from *konbu* (kelp) or *katsuobushi*. *Katsuobushi* is steamed and dried bonito (a dark oily fish) usually purchased as flakes and sprinkled on various dishes. Both *konbu* and *katsuobushi* are common gifts for special celebrations. *Nori* is a dried sheet of seaweed that can either be salty or plain. Plain *nori* is typically used for making *maki-zushi* (see page 96). *Wasabi* comes from the grated root of the *wasabi* plant. It is a very hot, bright green paste reputed to kill bacteria. It is usually eaten with *sashimi* (see page 98) or *soba* (see page 110) and is also a common condiment for *nigiri-zushi* (see page 96).

和食にはよく知られている食材がいくつかあります。だし、かつお節、のりやわさびなどです。

日本のだしは昆布、かつお節、（かつおは黒く、脂がのった魚）から作られるものが多いです。

かつお節は薫製して乾燥させたかつおで、普通は削ったものを買って、いろいろな料理にふりかけて使います。昆布とかつお節はお祝い事の贈り物にも広く使われています。のりは海藻を乾燥させたもので、塩味のものと味がついていないものがあります。味のない方ののりは巻き寿司を作る時に使います。

わさびはわさびという植物の根をすりおろしたものです。とても辛く鮮やかな緑色のペーストで、殺菌作用があると言われています。刺身やそばを食べる時、またにぎり寿司の薬味としても使われます。

- Making *katsuobushi* is similar to making a ham. It is made by smoking boiled bonito many times.

  かつお節の作り方はハムの作り方に似ています。ゆでたかつおを何度も薫製して作ります。

- *Nori* is made in a similar way to Japanese paper. The seaweed is chopped up and mixed with water, then spread out into a sheet and left to dry.

  のりの作り方は和紙の作り方に似ています。切り刻んだ海藻を水に溶かし、シート状に広げて乾燥させます。

- *Wasabi* is usually grated with a tool made from shark skin.

  わさびをおろす時には通常さめの皮でできたおろし器を使います。

- *Wasabi* comes as a powder or in a tube.

  粉わさびやチューブ入りのものも購入できます。

Katsuobushi

Wasabi

Nori

Konbu soup stock

SWEETS AND SNACKS | お菓子

キーワード	
sweets	甘いお菓子
pastry shell	（まんじゅうなどの）皮
filling	中身
dumpling	だんご
vegetable gelatin	寒天
a loaf of	ひとかたまりの

There are several popular sweets and snacks in Japan, including *manju*, *mochi* cakes, *dango*, *yokan*, *senbei* and *arare*.

Manju is a small sweet cake with a pastry shell made from flour, rice or buckwheat and a filling of sweet bean paste or sweet potato paste.

Mochi cakes are similar to *manju*, but have a *mochi* shell. There are seasonal variations of both *manju* and *mochi* cakes. Different ingredients are used and the cakes are presented differently. For example, in the spring, *mochi* cakes wrapped in leaves of the cherry tree are popular.

Dango is a skewer of three rice dumplings covered in a sweet bean paste or a soy sauce and sugar dip.

Yokan is made from sweet bean paste and vegetable gelatin. It looks a bit like a box-shaped loaf of jelly.

Senbei is a kind of cracker made from flour or rice. It usually has a salty or *shoyu* (see page 108) flavor.

Arare is similar to *senbei*, but is made from fried *mochi*.

日本には、まんじゅう、もち菓子、だんご、羊羹やせんべい、あられなど、甘いお菓子やスナックがいくつかあります。

まんじゅうは皮の部分が小麦粉、米粉、そば粉などでできていて、中身が小豆あんやさつまいもあんの、小さくて甘いケーキのようなお菓子です。

もち菓子はまんじゅうに似ていますが、もち皮でできています。まんじゅうやもち菓子は季節によっていろいろな種類があります。いろいろな材料が使われ、見た目も違います。例えば春には桜の木の葉で包んだもちが人気です。

だんごは3つの小さなだんごを串に刺し、小豆あんでくるんだり、砂糖醤油につけたものです。

羊羹は小豆あんと寒天などから作られています。箱形をしたゼリーのかたまりのようなものです。

せんべいは小麦粉や米でできたクラッカーの1種です。塩味か醤油味のものが多いです。

あられはせんべいに似ていますが、もちを揚げたものです。

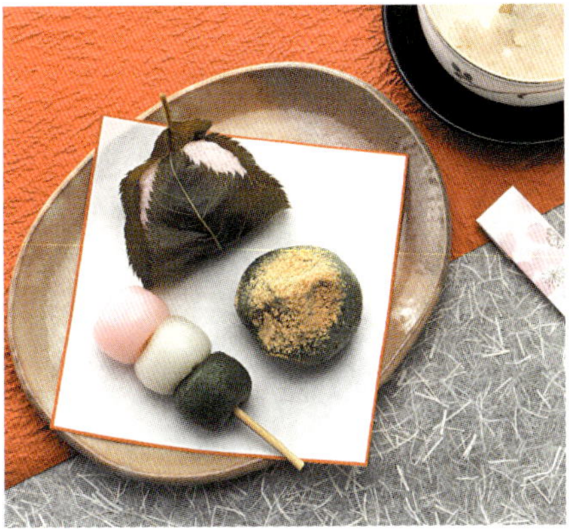
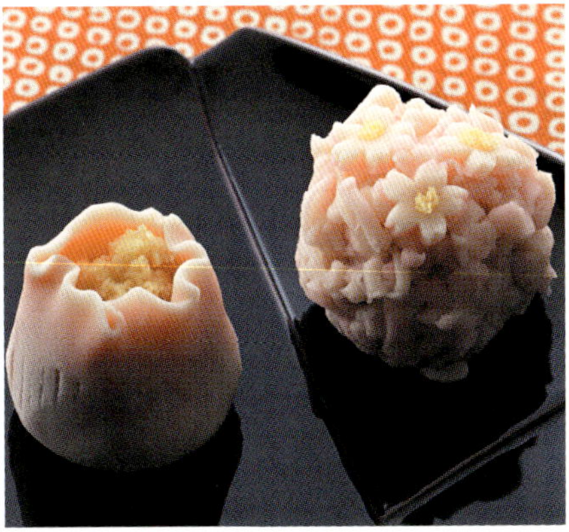
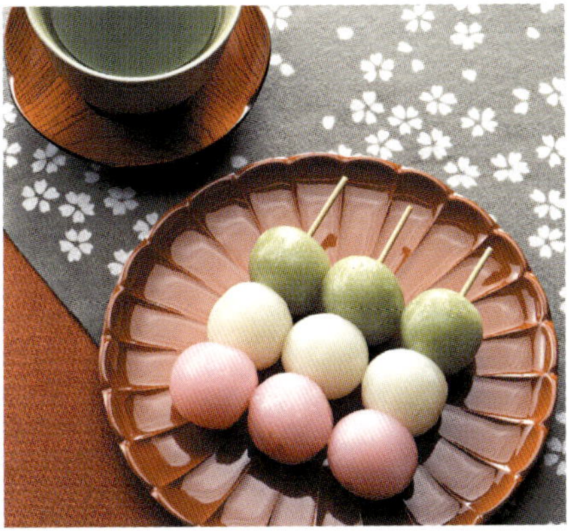
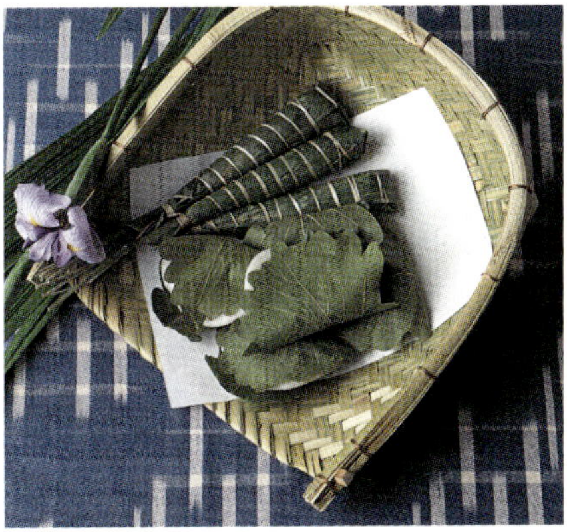
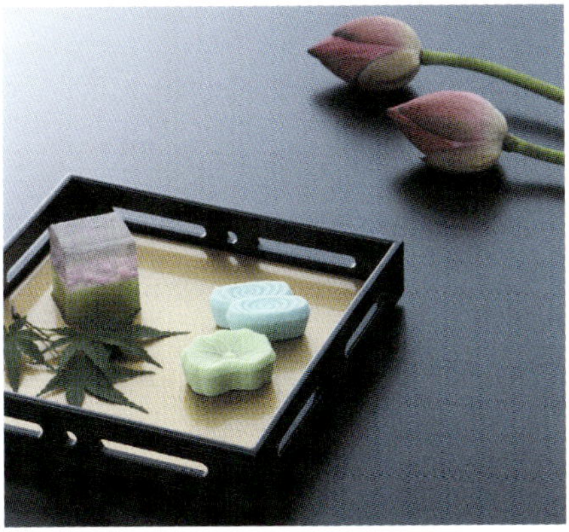
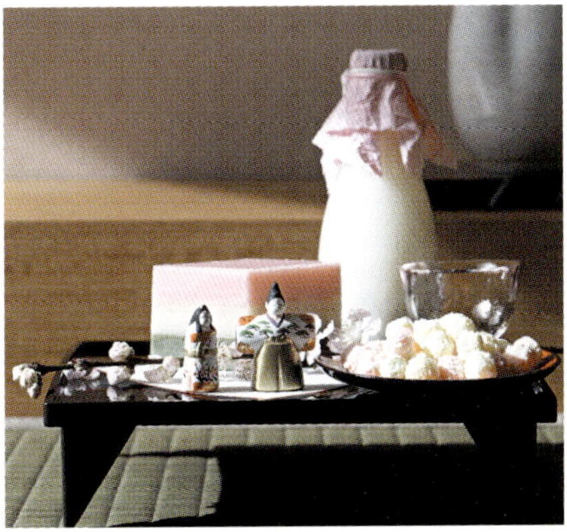

TEA お茶

キーワード	
unfermented	発酵していない
tea leaves	茶葉
black tea	紅茶
by contrast	対照的に
oolong tea	ウーロン茶

Tea came to Japan from China about 1,200 years ago and quickly became the most popular drink around. The most common tea in Japan is green tea, which is made from unfermented tea leaves. Western teas (i.e. black teas) by contrast, are made from fermented tea leaves, and oolong tea (popular in China) is made from half-fermented tea leaves. Green tea is always taken straight with no sugar or cream added and has been shown to have great health benefits. Japanese people take their green tea seriously and there are many brands of differing quality and price.

お茶は約1,200年前に中国から伝わったもので、すぐに広まりました。日本で最もよく飲まれるお茶は緑茶で、茶葉を発酵させずに作ります。対照的に欧米のお茶(紅茶)は茶葉を発酵させたもので、ウーロン茶(中国で一般的)は茶葉を半分発酵させたものです。緑茶は砂糖やミルクなどを入れずに飲み、健康にとても良いとされています。日本人は緑茶に関して思い入れが深く、このためいろいろな品質や価格の銘柄があります。

ALCOHOL | アルコール

キーワード

alcohol content
アルコール度

superior quality　上質の

spirit　蒸留酒

Although beer is common all across Japan these days, traditional Japanese alcohol is made from rice. The word sake in Japanese can be used to mean any type of alcohol, but it generally refers to a rice-based beverage with an alcohol content between twelve and twenty percent. Sake, just like wine, can be classified by its sweetness or dryness. The best sake is made in areas with superior quality water and rice. Sake can be served cold or warm, and is often used in cooking. It can be made at any time of year, but winter is the best, so most sake is produced in January or February.

Shochu refers to a group of spirits made from rice, wheat, buckwheat or sweet potato, and having an alcohol content of about twenty-five percent. It is usually made in the southern part of Kyushu, but also in Okinawa, where it is called *awamori*.

最近日本ではビールが多く飲まれていますが、昔ながらの日本の酒は米から作られています。日本語で酒と言えばあらゆるアルコール類を指すこともありますが、一般的にはアルコール度約12〜20度の、米から作られた酒を指します。ワインと同じように酒は甘口や辛口で分類されます。良い酒は上質の水と米が獲れる地域で作られます。酒は冷やでも燗でも飲まれ、料理にもよく使われます。1年を通して作ることは可能ですが、冬が1番良い時期で、ほとんどの酒は1月か2月に作られます。

焼酎は米、麦、そばやさつまいもなどから作られる蒸留酒で、アルコール度25度くらいです。南九州が主な産地ですが、沖縄でも泡盛という焼酎が作られています。

SHOGATSU | 正月

キーワード	
refer to	～のことを指す
be closed down	（店などが）休みになる
New Year's Eve	大晦日
pray for	～を祈る
steamed	蒸した
paste	ペースト/練り物
herring roe	ニシンの卵
sardine	イワシ
soy sauce	醤油
pea	豆
make certain	必ず～するようにする
last	持つ/足りる
customary	習慣的な
New Year's greeting card	年賀状
postcard	絵ハガキ
on the back	裏に
make sure	確実に～するように手配する
deliver	配達する
New Year's Day	元日

Shogatsu refers to the New Year period. January 1st is called *ganjitsu*, and the first three days of the New Year are called *sanganichi*. During these days many things are closed down. Japanese people often visit temples or shrines on New Year's Eve or during *sanganichi* to pray for happiness in the new year.

Special New Year's food called *osechi* is usually eaten at this time. *Osechi* includes *kamaboko* (steamed fish paste), *kazunoko* (herring roe), *gomame* (small dried sardines cooked in soy sauce and sugar) or *kuromame* (black peas). In the past all shops were closed during *sanganichi*, so families had to make certain they had enough food to last them for three days. It is customary to drink sake on New Year's Day.

Another New Year custom is the sending of New Year's greeting cards. Japanese New Year's cards are like postcards, and typically have a family picture and some family news on the back. Most people try to send their New Year's cards by December 25th to make sure they will be delivered on New Year's Day.

正月とは新年を迎えてからの一定の期間のことを指します。1月1日は元日、新年の最初の3日間は三が日と呼ばれます。この間はいろいろな機関が休みになります。日本人は大晦日か三が日の間に、新年の幸せを祈るため寺院や神社をお参りします。

正月にはおせちと呼ばれる正月用の特別な料理を食べます。おせちにはかまぼこ（魚のすり身を蒸したもの）、数の子（ニシンの卵）、ごまめ（小さな干しイワシを醤油と砂糖で調理したもの）や黒豆が入っています。昔、三が日の間は全ての店が休みだったので、各家庭で3日間は確実に持つだけの十分な料理を作らなければいけませんでした。元日にはお酒を飲む習慣があります。

また年賀状を送るのも新年の習慣の1つです。年賀状は絵ハガキのようなもので、裏には家族の写真が印刷されていたり、家族の近況が書かれていたりします。ほとんどの人は元日に確実に配達してもらうために12月25日までに年賀状を出すようにしています。

kuromame

kamaboko

gomame

kazunoko

COMING OF AGE DAY | 成人の日

キーワード

celebrate　祝う
adulthood　大人であること
previous year　前年
current year　本年
full citizen　成人
right to vote　選挙権
catch up with
　〜と近況を報告しあう

On this day Japanese people celebrate the adulthood of those who reach twenty between April 2nd of the previous year and April 1st of the current year. It is at this age that Japanese become full citizens and are given the right to vote. Each city or town has its own ceremony and it is often a good chance for these new adults to catch up with old friends. This holiday used to be on January 15th every year, but has recently been changed to the second Monday of January.

前年の4月2日から本年の4月1日までに20才を迎えた人が大人の仲間入りすることを祝う日です。日本では成人として認められ、選挙権が与えられるのが20才です。それぞれの市や町ごとに式典が催されるので、古い友だちと近況を報告しあう良い機会となっています。この祝日は以前は1月15日でしたが、今は1月の第2月曜日になっています。

SETSUBUN 節分

キーワード

used to 昔は〜だった
mark 示す
activity 行事
bean throwing 豆まき
throw まく
while 〜しながら
get out 出て行く
evil spirit 悪霊
demon 悪魔
scary 恐ろしい
fang 牙
horn 角
skin 肌
tiger fur shorts 虎の毛皮でできたパンツ
iron club 鉄の棍棒
designated good direction 決まった恵方
face (〜の方向に)向く
be supposed to 〜するはずである/〜することになっている

There used to be a special day to mark the changing of each season, but now there is only one, *setsubun*. This day, February 3rd, marks the end of winter and start of spring.

The most famous activity of *setsubun* is bean throwing. Beans are thrown out of the house while shouting, "*Oni wa soto!*" which means, "Get out evil spirits!" Beans are then thrown into the house while saying, "*Fuku wa uchi!*" meaning, "Come in good luck!" An *oni* is a kind of demon. They have scary faces with fangs and horns, and red or blue skin. They wear tiger fur shorts and carry iron clubs.

Each year has a designated good direction, and many people in the Kansai area eat *maki-zushi* (see page 96) while facing in that direction on *setsubun*. This is supposed to bring good luck.

昔はそれぞれの季節の変わり目を示す特別な日がありましたが、今ではたった1つ節分だけが残っています。この日、2月3日は冬が終わって春が始まる日とされています。

節分の最も有名な行事は豆まきです。「鬼は外!(悪霊出て行け)」と叫びながら、家の中から外へと豆をまきます。それから「福は内!(幸運入って来い)」と叫びながら、家の中へと豆をまきます。鬼とは悪魔のようなものです。恐ろしい顔をしていて牙と角をはやし、肌の色は赤や青です。虎の皮でできたパンツをはき、鉄の棍棒をかついでいます。

毎年決まった恵方があって、関西地方では節分の日にその方角に向かって巻き寿司を食べる人も多くいます。こうすると幸福が訪れると考えられています。

VALENTINE'S DAY/WHITE DAY | バレンタインデー/ホワイトデー

キーワード

in return	お返しとして
coworker	同僚
duty	義務
sign of affection	愛情の表現
approach	近づく
reserve	用意する
fill with	〜でいっぱいになる
make purchases	買い求める
tables are turned	立場が逆である
sales boost	売り上げ増加

Valentine's Day is celebrated a little differently in Japan. On February 14th, women give chocolate to men, but men give nothing in return. Girls give chocolate to their boyfriends or to boys they like, and wives give it to their husbands. Female workers also give it to their male coworkers, but this is called *giri choco* (duty chocolate) and isn't really a sign of affection. As Valentine's Day approaches, stores reserve large amounts of space to display chocolates and they fill with women making purchases.

Then, on March 14th, comes White Day and the tables are turned. On this day, boys and men who got chocolate give cookies or sweets in return. This day is unique to Japan and provides another large sales boost to stores.

日本のバレンタインデーは少し違った祝い方をします。2月14日に女性は男性にチョコレートを贈りますが、男性は何もお返ししません。女の子は恋人や好きな男の子に、妻は夫にチョコレートをプレゼントします。職場でも女性社員が同僚の男性にチョコレートをプレゼントしますが、これは義理チョコと呼ばれ、愛情の表現ではありません。バレンタインデーが近づくと店はチョコレートを山のように置くためのスペースを用意し、売場はチョコレートを買い求める女性でいっぱいになります。

3月14日のホワイトデーが来ると立場が逆になります。チョコレートをもらった男性はクッキーやキャンディーをお返しします。これは日本独特のもので、店はまた大きく売り上げをのばすことができます。

HINA MATSURI ひな祭り

キーワード

wish for ～を願う
display 飾る
middle 中間
put ~ away ～を片づける
soon after ～の後すぐに
be delayed 遅れる
three-tiered platform 3段飾り
the Emperor 男雛/天皇
the Empress 女雛/皇后
followed by その後に～が続く
eminent lord 大臣
servant 召使い
lantern 提灯
peach blossom 桃の花
diamond-shaped 菱形の
be offered to ～に供えられる

Hina Matsuri is held on March 3rd to wish for girls' health and safety and a happy marriage. Families with girls display *hina-ningyo* (*hina* dolls). They begin displaying them from the middle of February and put them away soon after March 3rd. If *hina-ningyo* are left on display too long, it is said that a girl's marriage will be delayed. A small set of *hina-ningyo* are displayed on a three-tiered platform, and a bigger set on a seven-tiered platform. *Dairibina* (the Emperor and the Empress) are on the top shelf followed by *sannin kanjo* (three ladies), *gonin bayashi* (five musicians), *udaijin* and *sadaijin* (two eminent lords), and three servants. Lanterns called *bonbori* and peach blossoms decorate the platforms. *Hishimochi* (diamond-shaped *mochi*, see page 112) and *shirozake* (white sweet sake) are offered to the dolls.

3月3日のひな祭りは、女の子の健やかな成長と幸せな結婚を願って行われます。女の子がいる家庭ではひな人形を飾ります。2月中頃から飾りを出し、3月3日が過ぎるとすぐに片づけます。ひな人形を長く飾りすぎると婚期が遅れると言われているからです。小型のひな人形セットは3段飾りで、大きなものは7段にもなります。1番上の段には内裏びな（男雛と女雛）、その下に三人官女、五人囃子、右大臣と左大臣、3人の召使いと続きます。ぼんぼりと呼ばれる提灯と桃の花も飾ります。菱餅と白酒も人形にお供えします。

HANAMI | 花見

キーワード

cherry blossom　桜の花
bloom　咲く
weather forecast　天気予報
rush　すぐに〜する
equal parts
　〜と同じようなもの
nature appreciation
　自然を楽しむこと
look up at　〜を見上げる
worry　心配事
temporary　はかない
rarely　ほとんど〜ない
yet　けれど

Every spring, usually around April, there is great excitement all across Japan. This excitement is caused by Japan's cherry blossom season. These beautiful pink flowers start blooming in the south and gradually move north. Every day people watch the weather forecast to see when cherry blossom season will reach their town. And when it does, they rush with their families, coworkers or friends to the nearest park to enjoy *hanami*. *Hanami* is equal parts picnic, party and nature appreciation. Groups of people gather under cherry trees and look up at the beautiful blossoms. While enjoying this view, and the warm spring weather, they drink beer and sake, eat snacks, and even sing karaoke.

At this special time of year everyone seems to have more energy. They can relax a bit and forget their worries. But unfortunately it is only temporary. Cherry blossoms rarely last more than two weeks in any one spot. Yet many people say that this is what makes them so special.

毎春、4月頃には日本中がうきうきした雰囲気につつまれます。桜の季節がやって来るからです。美しいピンク色の花は南から順に咲き始め、徐々に北へと向かいます。桜前線はいつ自分の住む町にたどり着くのかと、天気予報で毎日チェックします。そして開花すればすぐに家族や同僚、友人たちと近くの公園に花見に出かけます。花見はピクニックでありパーティーであり自然を楽しむものであります。グループで桜の木の下に集まり美しい花を見ます。桜景色と春の暖かさを楽しみながらビールや酒を飲んだり、食べたり、時にはカラオケを歌ったりもします。

1年のこの特別な時期には誰もが元気いっぱいに見えます。少しリラックスして心配事も忘れることができます。でも残念なことにこれははかないものにすぎません。どんな土地でも桜は2週間以上咲いていることはほとんどありません。けれど桜がはかないものだからこそこうも特別なのだと言う人もたくさんいます。

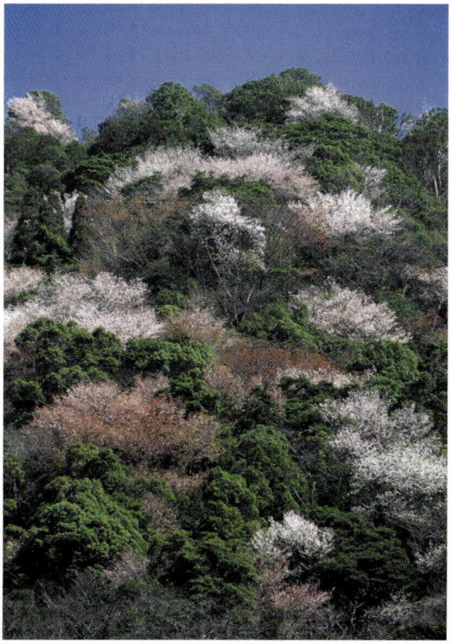

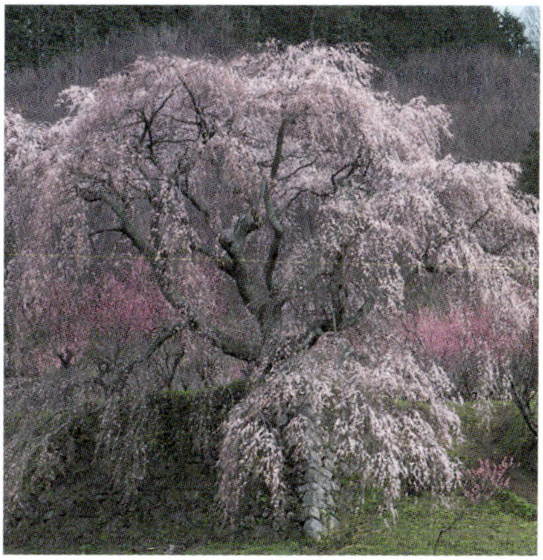

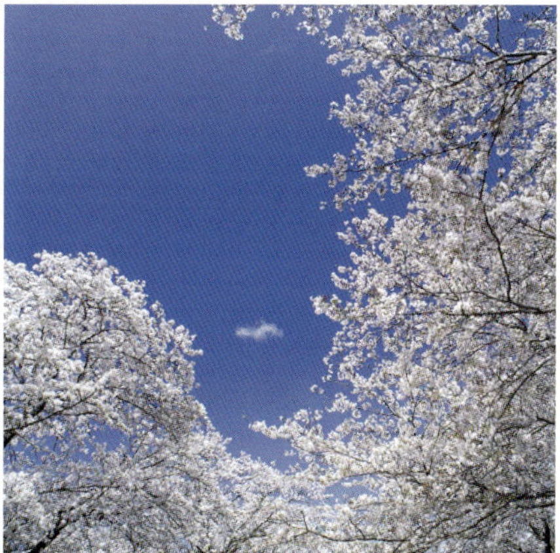

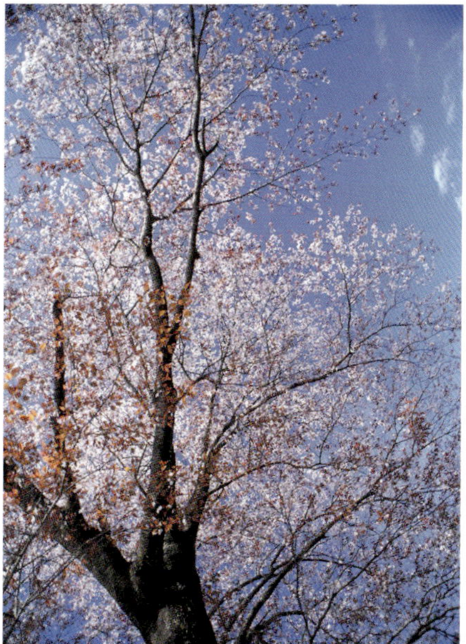

TANGO NO SEKKU | 端午の節句

キーワード
Children's Day　子どもの日
future success　将来の成功
fly *koinobori*
鯉のぼりをあげる
high up　高く
in armor　鎧をつけた
symbol　象徴
swim upriver
川を(泳いで)さかのぼる
represent　表す
symbolize　表す/象徴する
respectable　尊敬される

On May 5th, people celebrate *tango no sekku* (Children's Day), the boys festival. They wish for the good health and future success of boys. Families with sons fly *koinobori* (carp streamers) high up on a pole, or display *gogatsu-ningyo* (samurai dolls in armor). The carp is a symbol of success in life because it can swim upriver. Big carp streamers are three to four meters long and there are usually two or three on each pole. One is big and black and represents the father and the others are smaller and represent the children. The doll in armor is a symbol of the samurai, and symbolizes the parents' hopes that their children will be strong and respectable people.

5月5日は男の子の健やかな成長と将来の成功を祈って端午の節句を祝います。男の子がいる家庭では竿に鯉のぼりをつけて高くあげ、五月人形(鎧をつけた侍の人形)を飾ります。鯉は川をさかのぼることから出世の象徴とされています。大きな鯉のぼりは3、4メートルもあり、それぞれの竿にたいてい2つか3つの鯉がついています。大きくて黒いのは父親を表し、他のは小さく子どもたちを表します。鎧をつけた人形は侍を表し、子どもが強く尊敬される人間になるようにという親の願いを表しています。

GOLDEN WEEK | ゴールデンウィーク

キーワード

national holiday　祝日
former　前の
Emperor　天皇
Constitution Memorial Day
憲法記念日
close together
集中して/接近して
run from ~ through . . .
~から...まで続く

There are several national holidays around the beginning of May. The birthday of the former Emperor (Emperor Showa) on April 29th, Constitution Memorial Day on May 3rd, and Children's Day on May 5th. Because these holidays are so close together, most people are allowed a one-week holiday. This holiday was named Golden Week and now usually runs from April 29th through May 5th.

祝日が数日、5月の1週目あたりに集中しています。前天皇（昭和天皇）の誕生日が4月29日、憲法記念日が5月3日、そして子どもの日が5月5日です。休日が集中しているので1週間の休みを取ることができます。この期間の休みはゴールデンウィークと名づけられ、だいたい4月29日から5月5日の間になっています。

17	18	19	20	21	22	23
24	25	26	27	28	**29**	30
5/1	2	**3**	**4**	**5**	6	7

TANABATA 七夕

キーワード

origin 起源
legend 伝説
herder 牛飼い
weaver 機織り
become lazy 怠け者になる
heaven 天国/天
force ~ to . . . 〜に(無理矢理)...させる
opposite sides 両岸
the Milky Way 天の川
feel sorry for 〜を気の毒に思う
once a year 1年に1度
romantically ロマンティックに
imagine 想像する
paper strip 短冊
bamboo branch 笹の枝
shopping arcade 商店街
hanging from 〜から吊して

Tanabata's origin is the Chinese Star Festival which was introduced to Japan in the eighth century. It comes from a Chinese legend about Hikoboshi (Altair), the herder, and Orihime (Vega), the weaver. The two were hard working, but after they married they became lazy. The Emperor of Heaven got angry and forced them to live on opposite sides of the Milky Way. Orihime was so sad that she cried every day. The Emperor of Heaven felt sorry for them and allowed them to cross the Milky Way and meet once a year on the night of July 7th. On that night people can look up at the sky and romantically imagine that the two are crossing the Milky Way and meeting each other. Children write wishes on paper strips and decorate bamboo branches with them. Shopping arcades are also decorated on this day with colorful paper strips hanging from bamboo branches.

七夕の起源は8世紀に日本に紹介された中国の星の祭りです。これは牛飼いの彦星(アルタイル)と機織りの織姫(ベガ)についての中国の伝説に由来します。この2人は働き者でしたが、結婚してからは怠け者になってしまいました。天の帝はこのことに怒り、2人を天の川の両岸に別々に住ませました。織姫は悲しさのあまり毎日泣き暮らしました。天の帝は2人を気の毒に思い、1年に1度、7月7日の夜だけ天の川を渡って会うことを許しました。この夜には空を見上げ、2人が天の川を渡って会っているのだな、とロマンティックな想像をする人もいます。子どもたちは短冊に願いを書いて笹の枝に吊して飾ります。商店街も色紙を吊した笹飾りを作って飾りつけをします。

OBON お盆

キーワード

ancestor worship 先祖崇拝
at this time この時期に

Obon is a traditional Japanese holiday for ancestor worship. It usually runs from August 13th to 15th and many companies also have summer holidays at this time. Families usually gather together and visit the

grave	墓
spirit	霊
offering	お供え
place	置く
light	火を焚く
be floated down	浮かべて流す
departure	立ち去ること(帰って行くこと)

graves of their ancestors. It is believed that the spirits of their ancestors come back during *obon*. Many families have a *butsudan* (see page 48). During *obon*, offerings of fruit, flowers, and snacks are placed on the *butsudan*. In the past, small fires were lit in front of the house to welcome the spirits. In some areas, small boats with candles are floated down rivers to the sea on the evening of the 15th. This symbolizes the departure of the spirits back to heaven.

お盆は先祖を崇拝するための伝統的な日本の休日です。8月13日から15日で、この時期に多くの企業も夏休みに入ります。家族はたいてい集まり、先祖のお墓にお参りします。お盆の間に先祖の霊が帰って来ると信じられています。多くの家庭には仏壇があります。お盆の期間、くだもの、花、菓子などが仏壇に供えられます。昔は家の前で小さな火を焚き霊を迎え入れました。地方によっては15日の夜、ろうそくをともした小さな舟を海に続く川に浮かべて流す風習もあります。これは霊が天国に帰って行くことを表しています。

BON ODORI 盆踊り

キーワード	
calm	鎮める
tower	やぐら
participant	参加者
according to	〜によると
spirit of the dead	亡くなった人の霊
regional variation	地域独特の(踊り)/地域により変化に富んでいること

Bon odori is a traditional Japanese dance which is said to calm the spirits. It is one of the most important parts of *obon*. Typically, a tower is built and the participants dance around it. It is usually held at night when, according to tradition, spirits of the dead come back from heaven. There are regional variations throughout Japan.

盆踊りは日本の伝統的な踊りで霊を鎮めると言われています。これはお盆の最も大切な一部です。一般的にはやぐらが組まれて参加者はその廻りを踊ります。言い伝えによると亡くなった人の霊は夜に戻って来るので、たいてい夜に行われます。日本全国に地域独特の踊りがあります。

HANABI | 花火

キーワード

essential part　欠かせないもの
fireworks display　花火大会
date back to　〜にさかのぼる
skyrocket　打ち上げ花火
shoot into the sky
空に向かって打ち上げる
explode　炸裂する
fix　固定する
fountain　噴水
handheld　手で持てる
shoot sparks　火花を散らす
multi-colored　色とりどりの
fly out　飛び散る

Hanabi are an essential part of the Japanese summer. Large public displays are held all across Japan, and small family parties are also popular. Fireworks displays began in the Edo period (1603-1867) and quickly became popular. One of the most famous public displays today, at Sumida River in Tokyo, dates back to 1733.

There are three different types of *hanabi*. Skyrockets shoot into the sky and explode to look like large flowers. Ground fireworks are fixed on the ground and form different shapes like candles or fountains. The most popular one looks like Niagara Falls. Handheld fireworks shoot sparks from one end, but don't explode. Children love holding them and watching the multi-colored sparks fly out.

花火は日本の夏に欠かせないものです。日本各地で大きな花火大会が催されますし、家庭でできる小さな花火も人気があります。花火大会は江戸時代（1603年〜1867年）に始まり急速に広まりました。現在最も有名なものは東京の隅田川の花火大会で、その歴史は1733年にまでさかのぼります。

花火には3つの種類があります。打ち上げ花火は空に向かって打ち上げられ、巨大な花のように炸裂します。仕掛け花火は地面に固定され、ろうそくや噴水のようないろいろな形を作ります。最も有名なものはナイアガラの滝のように見えるものです。手で持てる花火は大きな音をたてて炸裂せず、先端から火花を散らします。子どもたちはこれを手に持って、色とりどりの火花が飛び散るのを眺めることが大好きです。

ENNICHI | 縁日

キーワード	
relate to	～にちなんだ
deities	仏様や神様
memorial service	供養
believer	信者
elderly people	お年寄り
divine favor	御利益
stall	屋台
set up	設ける/設置する

Ennichi are special days related to Buddhist or Shinto deities. On each day, small festivals or memorial services are held at temples or shrines. Believers offer snacks, fruit or money to the deities. Some elderly people believe that visiting temples and shrines on these days will bring them divine favor. On *ennichi* days food and game stalls are set up near temples and shrines. On summer evenings many people come to *ennichi* in *yukata* (see page 60).

縁日は仏教や神道の仏様や神様にちなんだ特別な日です。それぞれの日には、お寺や神社で小さなお祭りや供養が催されます。信者は仏様、神様に菓子、くだもの、お金などをお供えします。お年寄りの中にはこういった日にお寺や神社にお参りすると御利益があると信じている人もいます。縁日にはお寺や神社の近くに食べ物や遊びの屋台が設けられます。夏の夕方には浴衣を着て縁日にやって来る人もたくさんいます。

TSUKIMI | 月見

キーワード	
viewing	見ること
harvest festival	収穫祭
good rice crop	豊作
observe	見る/観察する
full moon	満月
lunar cycle	太陰周期
chestnut	栗
appreciation	鑑賞
look for	〜を探す
legendary	伝説の
mythical	神話的な
lunar	月の
dying	失われつつある

Tsuki means moon, and *tsukimi*, means moon viewing. Originally a harvest festival, *tsukimi* was a time to pray for a good rice crop. It was usually observed during a full moon in September, or sometimes October, depending on the lunar cycle. People would make offerings of *susuki* (Japanese pampas grass), *dango* (see page 120), chestnuts and sweet potatoes to the moon.

These days *tsukimi* is more about appreciation for the beauty of the moon. Children look for the legendary rabbit who lives on it. It is said that this mythical lunar rabbit makes *mochi* (see page 112) during the full moon. However, *tsukimi* is a dying tradition and is observed by fewer and fewer people each year.

月見は月を見るということです。元々は収穫祭で、月見は米の豊作を願うものでした。太陰周期によりますが、普通は9月または10月の満月を見ることが多かったようです。すすきやだんご、栗、さつまいもなどを月にお供えしました。

今日では月の美しさを鑑賞する意味合いが強くなっています。子どもたちは月に住んでいるという伝説のうさぎを探します。この神話的な月のうさぎは満月の日にもちをつくと言われています。しかし、月見は失われつつある伝統で、月見をする人は年々減っています。

SPORTS DAY | 体育の日

キーワード

in memory of　〜を記念して
field day　運動会
compete against
〜と競争する/競い合う
event　種目
tug-of-war　綱引き
grade　学年
be assigned to
〜に割り当てられる
join in　〜に参加する

Originally held on October 10th in memory of the 1964 Summer Olympics in Tokyo, Sports Day is now held on the second Monday of October. Some schools have a field day around this time. Teams compete against each other in several events, such as *tamaire* (throwing balls into a basket), *tsunahiki* (like tug-of-war), relay races, and dancing.

Japanese schools typically have several classes for each grade. For example there may be an A, B, and C class for each grade. Sports Day teams are formed by putting the A classes from all the grades together, the B classes together, and so on. Students from each team are assigned to compete in each event. Sports Day is also a family event, as parents usually come to watch their kids compete. Parents can even join in some events.

体育の日は元々は1964年の東京オリンピックの記念として10月10日に制定されていましたが、今では10月の第2月曜日になっています。学校によってはこの時期に運動会を開きます。チーム対抗で玉入れ（かごにボールを投げ入れる）、綱引き、リレーやダンスなど、いろいろな種目をで競い合います。

日本の学校はたいてい1学年に何クラスかあります。例えば各学年にA、B、Cの3クラスがあるとします。運動会では各学年の全てのAクラス、全てのBクラスをひとまとめにしたチームが作られます。それぞれのチームの生徒は各種目で競い合うよう割り当てられます。運動会は家族行事でもあり、両親は子どもたちを見にやって来ます。両親が参加できる競技もあります。

SHICHI-GO-SAN 七五三

キーワード

manner of dress　服装
grow older
大きくなる/年を取る
no longer　もう～ない
growth　成長
local　近くの
priest　神主
continued development
変わらぬ成長

Long ago it was customary for children to change their hairstyle and manner of dress as they grew older. Although this tradition is no longer observed, the Japanese continue to celebrate the growth of their children with the *Shichi-Go-San* Festival. *Shichi-Go-San* means seven-five-three. On November 15th boys of three and five and girls of three and seven dress up in traditional kimono and visit a local shrine. Parents make offerings at the shrine and the priest prays for the continued development of their children.

昔は子どもたちが大きくなるにつれ、髪型や服装を変える習慣がありました。もうこの伝統はなくなってしまいましたが、七五三の日に子どもの成長を祝い続けています。七五三は7、5、3ということです。11月15日には3才と5才の男の子、3才と7才の女の子が着物を着て近くの神社にお参りします。両親は神社にお供えをして、神主は子どもの変わらぬ成長を祈ります。

OMISOKA 大晦日

キーワード

goldsmith 金細工職人
buckwheat そば粉
dough 粉を練ったもの
refuse gold dust 金のくず
workshop 仕事場
grow the idea 〜という考えが生まれる
wealth 富
stay up all night 一晩中起きている
become less common すたれる
desire 煩悩/欲望
overcome 克服する
strike (鐘を)つく
remove 消し去る
manage to なんとか〜する

The last day of the year is called *omisoka*. On *omisoka* people finish cleaning their houses to welcome in the new year and eat *soba* (see page 110). In the past Japanese goldsmiths used buckwheat dough to collect refuse gold dust in their workshops. From this grew the idea that *soba* brings wealth and that to eat *soba* would bring good luck or success. People used to stay up all night on *omisoka* to welcome the god of New Year, but this is becoming less common now. Many people do however visit Buddhist temples on this night. Buddhists believe that we have 108 desires that we must overcome. On *omisoka* each Buddhist temple rings its bell 108 times. Each striking of the bell is believed to remove one desire. Those who do manage to stay up all night often climb to the top of a mountain or go to the beach to see the first sunrise of the year.

1年の最後の日は大晦日と呼ばれます。大晦日には新しい年を迎えるために家中のそうじをすませ、そばを食べます。昔の金細工職人は、仕事場に飛び散った金のくずを集めるのにそば粉を練ったものを使っていました。このためそばは富をもたらし、食べると幸運と成功ももたらすという考えが生まれました。昔は大晦日の夜には新年の神様を迎えるために一晩中起きていましたが、今ではこの風習もすたれています。しかし、この日の夜にお寺にお参りする人はたくさんいます。仏教では人間には108つの克服すべき煩悩があるとされています。大晦日にはどのお寺でも鐘が108回つかれます。1回1回の鐘の音が煩悩を1つずつ消し去ると考えられています。一晩中がんばって起きている人の中には初日の出を見るために山の頂上に登ったり、海岸に行く人もいます。

WEDDINGS 婚礼

キーワード

get married 結婚する
permission 許し/許可
as well その上
go-between 仲人/仲介者
decide on 〜を決める
wedding date 結婚式の日取り
boss 上司
serve 務める
additional 付加的な
avoid 避ける
groom 花婿
prepare for 〜の準備をする
religion 宗教
bride 花嫁
consider みなす
secular public ceremony 非宗教的な式(人前式)
cosmetic 形だけの
followed by 後に〜が続いて
reception 披露宴
attend 出席する
relatives 親戚

Once a couple decides to get married, the man visits the woman's house to get permission from her parents. After receiving permission, the man visits the woman's parents again, this time with his parents as well. Together they choose a *nakodo* (a go-between) and decide on a wedding date. The *nakodo* is usually an older married person who the man knows. The man generally asks his boss to be the *nakodo*. The *nakodo*'s wife serves as an additional *nakodo*. The actual wedding date is often chosen to avoid traditionally unlucky days. About six months before the wedding a ceremony called *yuino* is held. At this time, the *nakodo* hands money or goods from the groom to the woman's family to help prepare for the wedding.

結婚する当人同士が結婚を決めたら、男性は両親から結婚の許しをもらうために女性の家を訪問します。許しを得た後、男性は女性の家をもう1度訪問します。この時は自分の両親も連れて行きます。そこで両家は仲人を選び、結婚式の日取りを決めます。仲人は普通、男性の知り合いで年齢が上の既婚者がなります。自分の上司に仲人をお願いすることが多いようです。仲人の奥さんも一緒に夫婦で仲人を務めます。結婚式の日取りは縁起の悪い日を避けて選ばれます。結婚式の半年ほど前に結納という儀式があります。この時、仲人は花婿から預かった結婚の準備のお金と品物を女性の家族に手渡します。

These days, the religion of the bride and groom isn't usually considered very important. The style of ceremony may be Buddhist, Shintoist, Christian, or a secular public ceremony, but the choice is mostly cosmetic. Recently, Christian style weddings at hotel chapels have become popular. The ceremony is then followed by a reception held in the same hotel. Some guests attend both the ceremony and the reception, and some attend only the reception. During the reception, the couple's friends, bosses, or relatives give speeches, or sometimes sing songs. The bride often changes her clothes once or twice during the reception. Another option that has become popular recently is simply to have a reception at a restaurant. Some time after the wedding day most couples go somewhere nice for their honeymoon.

最近では花婿、花嫁の宗教はあまり問題にならないようです。式のスタイルは仏前、神前、キリスト教式や人前式などがありますが、どの式のスタイルを選んでも宗教的な意味合いはなく形だけのものです。最近ではホテルのチャペルでのキリスト教式の結婚式が一般的です。式の後に同じホテルで披露宴が行われます。招待客の中には式と披露宴の両方に出席する人や披露宴だけに出席する人がいます。披露宴ではカップルの友人、上司や親戚がスピーチをしたり時には歌を歌ったりします。花嫁が、1、2度お色直しをすることがよくあるようです。その他の最近の傾向としては、レストランでシンプルに披露宴を行うことも流行しています。結婚式が終わってしばらくするとほとんどのカップルは新婚旅行に出かけます。

PRESENTS | 贈り物

キーワード

occasion	機会
graduation	卒業
move into	～に引っ越す
get sick	病気になる
enter school	入学する
reach	達する
certain ages	一定の年齢
client	顧客
maintain	続ける
value	相場/金額
detergent	洗剤
gift certificate	商品券
advertising	宣伝する
leading up to	～までの
gifts of money	祝儀
envelope	封筒
string	ひも
high quality	上等の
amount of money	金額
depend on	～による
relationship	関係
recipient	受け手

Japanese people give gifts on many of the same occasions as in the West. For example, for birthdays, graduations and weddings as well as when someone has a baby, moves into a new house or gets sick. However, they also give gifts for entering school, getting a job, and reaching certain ages. In addition, there are two seasonal gift-giving events, *chugen* and *seibo*. *Chugen* is a summer gift, usually given in July or August. *Seibo* is a winter gift given in December. Both are usually given to one's boss, clients or teachers as a way to maintain good relations. The value of the gift is usually between ¥3,000 and ¥5,000. Popular gifts are beer, detergent, soap, food or gift certificates. Many commercials advertising *chugen* and *seibo* are broadcast on TV in the weeks leading up to these seasons and department stores have sales at this time.

For gifts of money, a special envelope with a fancy ribbon is used. The ribbon usually has red and white strings. For special occasions, such as weddings, high quality envelopes are used. The amount of money given depends on the occasion, and the relationship between giver and recipient.

日本人も欧米と同じような機会に贈り物をします。誕生日、卒業、結婚式などの他に、赤ちゃんが生まれた時、新しい家に引っ越した時、病気になった時などにもです。また一方で子どもが入学した時、就職した時や一定の年齢に達した時にも贈り物をします。さらに、中元や歳暮といった季節の贈り物をする習慣が2つあります。中元は夏の贈り物で、7月や8月に贈られます。歳暮は12月に贈られる冬の贈り物です。両方とも良いお付き合いを続けるために上司、顧客、先生などに贈ります。贈り物の相場は3,000円から5,000円です。人気のある贈り物はビール、洗剤、石けん、食品、商品券などです。シーズンまでの期間は中元や歳暮を宣伝するコマーシャルがテレビで流れ、デパートはこの時期にセールをします。

御祝儀を贈る時はリボンのついた専用の封筒が使われます。リボンは通常紅白です。結婚式のような特別な機会には上等の封筒が使われます。金額はその時や送り手と受け手の関係により違います。

145

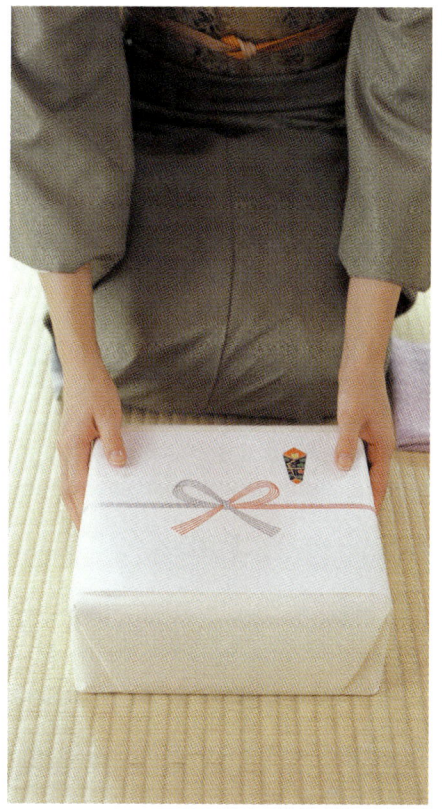

JAPANESE WRITING 日本の文字

キーワード

writing system	表記法
ideography	表意文字
character	文字
represent	表す
over the years	長い年月をかけて
combine with	～と組み合わさる
form	形作る
phonetic writing system	表音文字
phonetic syllable	音節
rather than	むしろ
vowel sound	母音
consonant sound	子音
remaining	残りの
identical	全く同じ
primarily	主として/そもそも
loan word	外来語
elementary school	小学校
in multiple ways	何通りもの
exact	正確な
guess	読み取る/推測する
context	前後関係
empty	空っぽの
spelling	スペル/綴り

Japanese has three writing systems, *kanji*, *hiragana* and *katakana*. *Kanji* is a form of ideography (each character represents one word) which was invented in China. It was introduced to Japan some time before the fifth century and is still used today. Over the years, some characters have combined with other characters to form new words. Although many of the basic characters are still the same in China and Japan, the meanings of some have changed slightly over time. In the ninth century, Japan invented two phonetic writing systems, *hiragana* and *katakana*. They are like alphabets, but each character represents a phonetic syllable, rather than a single sound. *Hiragana* and *katakana* each contain forty-six characters. Five of the characters represent the five vowel sounds used in Japanese. One character represents a single consonant sound which is a cross between m and n. And the remaining forty characters represent various consonant vowel combinations. *Hiragana* and *katakana* represent identical sounds, but use different characters. The main reason for having two sets is that one of them, *katakana*, is used primarily to write loan words (i.e. words from other countries).

日本語には3つの表記法があります。漢字、ひらがな、カタカナです。漢字は表意文字（1文字で1つの単語を表す）で、中国で発明されました。5世紀以前に日本に伝えられ、今日でも使われています。長い年月をかけて、他の漢字と組み合わさって違う単語を形作ったものもあります。基本的な漢字は中国の漢字と同じですが、中には時代とともに意味が少し違ってきているものもあります。9世紀になってひらがなとカタカナの2つの表音文字が発明されました。これらはアルファベットと似ていますが、それぞれの文字が1つの音節を表します。(日本語をローマ字表記すると例えば「ま」は ma と表されます。英語ではこれは m と a が組み合わさった、1つの音節を表していると考えます) ひらがなとカタカナは46文字あります。そのうち5つの文字が日本語の母音を表します。（「あいうえお」のこと）また n と m の間の子音を表す文字が1つあります。（「ん」のこと）残りの40文字が子音と母音が組み合わさった音です。ひらがなとカタカナは全く同じ音を表しますが、表記は違います。この2つの表記法が使われている理由の1つは、カタカナが主に外来語を表すために使われるからです。

Hiragana and *katakana* are much simpler to learn than *kanji*. Children learn these characters first, and children's books are usually written in *hiragana*. Kids do learn *kanji* from the first year of elementary school, but they start with simple ones. Some *kanji* characters can be read in multiple ways, and the exact meaning must sometimes be guessed from the context. For example, 空 could mean sky or empty. This is similar to words in English which have the same spelling but different meanings (light, hot, etc.).

ひらがなとカタカナは漢字よりもずっと覚えやすいです。子どもはまずひらがなとカタカナを先に学びます。子ども向けの本はほとんどがひらがなで書かれています。小学校1年生で漢字を習い始めますが、簡単なものから習います。漢字の中には何通りにも読めるものがあるので、正確な意味を前後関係から読みとらないといけないこともあります。例えば「空」は空という意味と、空っぽという意味があります。これは同じスペルで意味が違う英単語と似ています。(light：明るい、軽いなど、hot：暑い、辛いなど)

あ ア

hiragana　　*katakana*

THE JAPANESE SYLLABARY 五十音表

あア a	いイ i	うウ u	えエ e	おオ o
かカ ka	きキ ki	くク ku	けケ ke	こコ ko
さサ sa	しシ shi	すス su	せセ se	そソ so
たタ ta	ちチ chi	つツ tsu	てテ te	とト to
なナ na	にニ ni	ぬヌ nu	ねネ ne	のノ no
はハ ha	ひヒ hi	ふフ fu	へヘ he	ほホ ho

hiragana → あ ア ← katakana
a ← sound

ま マ ma	み ミ mi	む ム mu	め メ me	も モ mo
や ヤ ya		ゆ ユ yu		よ ヨ yo
ら ラ ra	り リ ri	る ル ru	れ レ re	ろ ロ ro
わ ワ wa				を ヲ wo
ん ン n				

BASIC JAPANESE PHRASES | 簡単な日本語フレーズ

Hi./Hello./Good afternoon.	こんにちは。 Konnichiwa.	
Nice to meet you.	はじめまして。 Hajimemashite.	
Good morning.	おはようございます。 Ohayogozaimasu.	
Good evening.	こんばんは。 Konbanwa.	
Good night.	お休みなさい。 Oyasuminasai.	
Good bye.	さようなら。 Sayonara.	
See you.	またね。 Matane.	
Thank you.	ありがとう。 Arigato.	
You're welcome.	どういたしまして。 Doitashimashite.	
Excuse me./I'm sorry.	ごめんなさい。 Gomennasai.	
I'm Tanaka Hanako.	私は田中花子です。 Watashiwa Tanaka Hanako desu.	
Yes.	はい。 Hai.	
No.	いいえ。 Iie.	
Please.	お願いします。 Onegaishimasu.	
Okay.	いいですよ。 Iidesuyo.	
Where are you from?	どちらのご出身ですか？ Dochirano goshusshin desuka?	

I'm from Japan.	私は日本の出身です。 Watashiwa Nihon no shusshindesu.
Where do you live?	どちらにお住まいですか？ Dochirani osumai desuka?
I live in Osaka.	私は大阪に住んでいます。 Watashiwa Osakani sundeimasu.
This is my father.	こちらは私の父です。 Kochirawa watashino chichidesu.
What's wrong?	どうしましたか？ Doshimashitaka?
What's this?	これは何ですか？ Korewa nandesuka?
Would you like some?	（食べ物などを勧めて）いかがですか？ Ikagadesuka?
How lucky!	ついてますね。 Tsuitemasune.
That's cool.	すごいですね。 Sugoidesune.
How nice!	素敵！ Suteki.
I'm happy.	嬉しいです。 Ureshiidesu.
I'm excited.	わくわくします。 Wakuwaku shimasu.
That's too bad.	お気の毒に。 Okinodokuni.
I'm disappointed.	残念です。 Zannendesu.
Really?	本当ですか？ Hontodesuka?
That's right.	そうですね。 Sodesune.

ORIGAMI | 折り紙

キーワード

fold ~ in half　～を半分に折る
triangle　三角形
crease　折り目をつける
reopen　もう1度開く
diagonally　斜めに
top layer　上の側
at the bottom of　～の下側に
complete　完成した

A dog's face　犬の顔

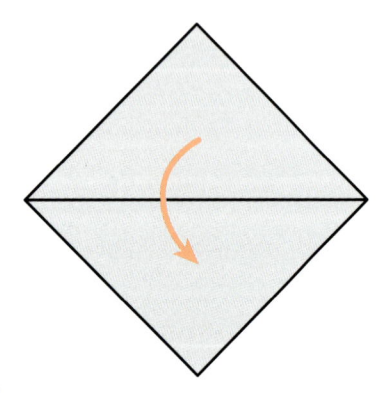

1.
Fold the paper in half to make a triangle.
紙を半分に折って三角形を作ります。

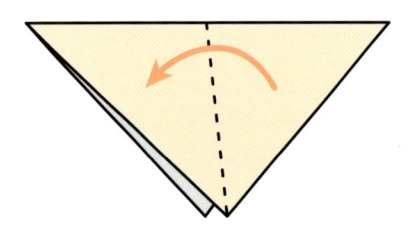

2.
Fold the triangle in half again, crease it, and reopen.
三角形をもう半分に折り、真ん中に折り目をつけてもう1度広げます。

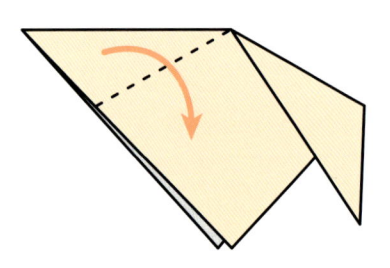

3.
Fold the right and left corners down diagonally to make the dog's ears.
上の方の左右を斜めに折り曲げて犬の耳を作ります。

4.

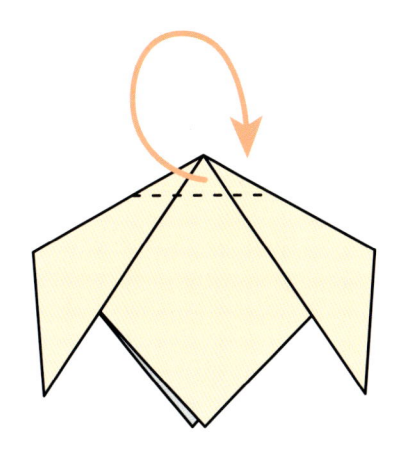

Fold the top corner back.

上の部分を後ろ側に折ります。

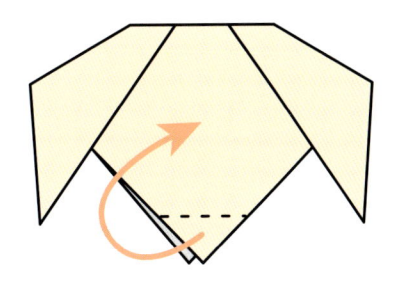

5.

Fold the top layer of paper at the bottom of the triangle up just a little to make the dog's mouth.

三角形の上の紙の下側をほんの少し折って犬の口を作ります。

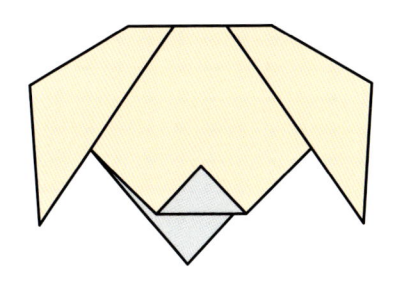

6.

Draw eyes and a nose if you wish and the dog's face is complete.

目と鼻を描き入れても良いです。さあ、犬の顔のでき上がりです。

OMAMORI｜お守り

キーワード

good luck charm　幸運を招くチャーム/お守り
invocation　祈願
a piece of　一切れの/1枚の
wood　木
wrap　包む
pouch　小袋
cloth　布
suit one's needs　ニーズに合う/要求を満たす
traffic safety　交通安全
examination　試験
easy childbirth　安産
hang　吊す

Omamori are small good luck charms sold at temples and shrines. Invocations and the names of gods, shrines or temples are written on a small piece of wood or paper and wrapped in a pouch made of brightly colored cloth. People buy the charm which suits their needs: there are some for traffic safety, success in school examinations, success in business, good health and for easy childbirth. People usually hang their charms on their bags, in their cars or at home.

お守りはお寺や神社で売られている幸運を招くチャームのことです。祈願や、神様、神社、寺院の名前が小さな木片や紙切れに書かれていて、明るい色の布袋に包まれています。それぞれ自分の願い事に合うお守りを買います。交通安全、合格祈願、商売繁盛、健康、安産などがあります。バッグに吊したり、車の中に吊したり、家の中に置いたりしています。

MANEKINEKO｜招き猫

キーワード

figurine　置物
approximately　～くらい/およそ
pose　格好をする
front paw　前脚
raise　上げる
beckon　招き寄せる
in hopes of　～を期待して
attract　招き寄せる
customer　客
prosperous　繁盛している

Manekineko are cat figurines that first became popular approximately two hundred years ago. They pose with one front paw raised to beckon people. This gesture means "come here" in Japan, so shops, restaurants, and hotels display them in hopes of attracting customers and making their businesses prosperous. If the right paw is raised, it brings money. If the left paw is raised, it brings customers. The higher the paw is raised, the more fortune it will bring.

招き猫は猫の置物で、200年ほど前に初めて流行しました。招き猫は前脚を上げて、人を招き寄せる格好をしています。このしぐさは日本では

「こっちにいらっしゃい」という意味なので、商店、レストラン、旅館などが客を招き寄せ、商売繁盛を期待して飾ってあります。右脚を上げているとお金を招き、左脚を上げていると客を招きます。上げている脚が高いほど、より多くの福を招くと言われています。

DARUMA｜だるま

キーワード

papier-mache　張り子の
monk　僧
found　開祖する
Zen sect　禅宗
legend　言い伝え
continuous　ずっと/連続的な
meditation　瞑想
come true　叶う/実現する
weight　重くする
bounce back　起きあがる
knocked over　ひっくり返される
be knocked down　倒される

A *daruma* is a small, round papier-mache doll that is said to represent the Indian monk who founded the Zen sect. Legend says that he became unable to walk because he sat in continuous meditation for nine years. For about two hundred years the *daruma* has been considered a good luck charm for success in either life or in business. Nowadays, they are sometimes used to wish for other things such as successfully passing examinations. *Daruma* are painted red, except for the face, and don't usually have the eyes painted in. When wishing for something, people paint in one eye. If the wish comes true, they paint in the other. The bottoms of *daruma* are weighted and bounce back by themselves when knocked over. Even if they are knocked down many times, they always bounce back, so they are a symbol of never giving up.

だるまは小さくて丸い張り子の人形で、禅宗を開祖したインド人の僧がモデルだと言われています。その僧は9年間も座ったままずっと瞑想をしていたので、歩けなくなってしまったという言い伝えがあります。だるまは200年ほど前から、開運出世、商売繁盛のお守りとされています。現在では合格祈願のような他の願い事をする時にも使われます。だるまは顔以外は赤く、普通は目が描かれていません。願い事をする時に目を1つ描き入れ、願いが叶うともう1つの目を描き入れます。底を重くしてあるので、ひっくり返しても自分で起きあがります。何度倒れても必ず起きあがることから、決してあきらめないという象徴になっています。

UCHIWA/SENSU | 団扇/扇子

キーワード	
bamboo	竹
frame	（団扇の）骨
round in shape	丸い形の
originate in	～で始まる
logo	ロゴ
hand ~ out	～を配る
busy	人の多い
public place	公共の場
folding	折り畳みの
spoke frame	（扇子の）骨
creased	折り目のついた
fold up	折り畳む
push together	閉じる/くっつける
surface	表面

Uchiwa and *sensu* are both types of fan. *Uchiwa* have bamboo or plastic frames covered with paper and are basically round in shape.

Pictures are usually painted or printed on *uchiwa*. This style of fan originated in China and came to Japan some time in the eighth century. These days it is often used as a kind of advertising in the summer. Stores and companies make *uchiwa* with their company name and logo. They then hand them out to people in front of train stations or other busy public places. People often use *uchiwa* to keep cool at summer festivals.

団扇と扇子はファンの1種です。団扇は竹やプラスチック製の骨に紙を貼ったもので、たいていは丸い形をしています。
団扇には絵が描かれたり、印刷されたりしていることがよくあります。この種のファンは元々は中国で作られていて、日本には8世紀頃に伝えられました。最近では夏に広告の1つとしてよく利用されています。店や企業などが社名やロゴをつけて団扇を作り、駅前や人の多い場所で配ったりします。夏祭りの時に団扇を使って涼む人もたくさんいます。

Sensu are much fancier and more formal. They are folding fans with a wood spoke frame. The spokes of the frame are connected at one end with a pin. The frame is covered with creased paper. It is designed to fold up when the spokes are pushed together. This makes *sensu* compact and easy to carry. Originally, they were used not just to fan oneself, but also as a writing surface. People wrote poems on them, decorated them with pictures and colorful string, and sent them to people as gifts. They are often carried as an accessory when wearing a kimono. They are also sometimes used for traditional Japanese dances or during noh and *kyogen* plays.

扇子はよりしゃれていてフォーマルな感じです。扇子は木製の骨でできた折り畳みのファンです。骨は一方の端がピンで留められています。骨は折り目のついた紙で覆われていて、骨を閉じると折り畳めるようにデザインされています。このため扇子は小さく畳め、持ち運びが便利です。元々はあおぐためだけでなく、表面に書き物をするために使われていました。和歌を書いたり、絵や色鮮やかなひもで飾ったりして贈り物として使うこともありました。着物を着た時の小物としても使います。また伝統的な日本舞踊や能、狂言でも使われることがあります。

WASHI 和紙

キーワード

centralization	中央集権化
government	政府
increased	増大した
bureaucracy	官僚支配
demand for	～に対する需要
material	原料
bark	樹皮
fiber	繊維
shrub	灌木
absorbent	吸水性がある
translucent	半透明の
pressed leaves	押し葉
be embedded in	～に埋め込まれる

Paper was introduced to Japan sometime around the seventh century. The centralization of the government and increased bureaucracy of the Nara period (710-784), led to a big increase in demand for paper. Traditional Japanese paper is handmade and is very different from normal paper. Several types have evolved over the centuries, but the main materials for *washi* come from the bark fibers of shrubs. Japanese paper is strong, absorbent and translucent; and pressed leaves or flowers are sometimes embedded in the paper to add to its beauty.

日本に紙が伝えられたのは7世紀頃です。奈良時代(710年～784年)に政府の中央集権化と官僚支配が強まったため、紙の需要が急速に増えました。伝統的な日本の和紙は手漉きで、普通の紙とは違います。また何世紀もの間にいろいろな種類の和紙が作られました。和紙の主原料は灌木の樹皮繊維です。和紙は強く、吸水性があり、半透明です。押し葉や押し花を埋め込んだ、より美しい和紙もあります。

NOREN のれん

キーワード

split	切れ目の入った
strand	（より合わせた）ひも
twisted	ねじれた
establishment	店舗/旅館、会社などの施設
divider	仕切

A *noren* is a type of split curtain usually hung from the entrance of shops or restaurants. Some *noren* are made of a single piece of cloth with two or three slits. Others are made from several strands of twisted rope. The name of the establishment or type of business is often printed on the curtain. Traditionally, *noren* showed that a shop or restaurant was open for business. Nowadays, some people use *noren* in their homes as room dividers or just for decoration.

のれんは店やレストランの入口にかかっている切れ目の入ったカーテンのようなもののことです。1枚の布に2、3の切れ目が入ったのれんや、よった綱をいくつもたらして作ったのれんなどがあります。のれんには店舗名や業種名がよく染め抜かれています。のれんがかけられていたら店やレストランは営業中ということですが、最近では家庭で部屋の仕切やインテリアとして使っている人もいます。

TENUGUI | 手ぬぐい

キーワード

souvenir　おみやげ

pattern　柄

A common gift or souvenir, a *tenugui* is a bit like a bandana. It's a small cotton cloth used as a towel or worn on the head. Traditionally, they were white with patterns printed in blue ink, but now there are many more colorful *tenugui*. Men typically wear *tenugui* during festivals, twisting them into a ring shape and wearing them around their necks or heads.

手ぬぐいはバンダナに似たもので、プレゼントやおみやげとしてよく贈られます。小さな木綿の布で、タオルとして使ったり頭に巻いたりします。元々は白地に柄を藍色で染めたものが多かったのですが、最近ではカラフルな手ぬぐいがたくさんあります。男性は祭りの時に手ぬぐいを輪のような形にねじて首や頭に巻きます。

改訂版　ホームステイ英会話　おみやげ本
　　　　　　　2005年7月10日　初版発行
　　　　　　　2006年1月20日　第2刷発行

企画・編集・制作	株式会社ジオス 教材開発研究室
発行所	株式会社ジオス
営業所	141-0032 東京都品川区大崎1丁目6番4号
	新大崎勧業ビルディング4F
	TEL:03-5434-2831　FAX:03-5434-2833
編集室	770-0944 徳島県徳島市南昭和町1丁目48-1
	TEL:088-625-7807　FAX:088-655-5915

表紙デザイン	如月舎
イラスト	浅羽壮一郎
印刷	東洋紙業株式会社

ISBN4-86109-024-5　C0082
©GEOS Corporation 2005
Printed in Japan